ATTP 3-97.11/MCRP 3-35.1D (FM 31-70 and FM 31-71)

Cold Region Operations

JANUARY 2011

Headquarters, Department of the Army

Published by Books Express Publishing
Books Express Publishing, 2011
ISBN 978-1-78039-962-1

Books Express publications are available from all good retail and online booksellers. For publishing proposals and direct ordering please contact us at: info@books-express.com

ATTP 3-97.11/MCRP 3-35.1D (FM 31-70 and FM 31-71), C1

Change No. 1

Headquarters
Department of the Army
Washington, DC, 10 June 2011

Cold Region Operations

1. This change rescinds paragraphs 2-63 through 2-66 and re-numbers paragraphs 2-67 through 2-82 for consecution.

2. ATTP 3-97.11/MCRP 3-35.1D, 28 January 2011, is changed as follows:

Remove Old Pages	Insert New Pages
pages i through ii	pages i through ii
pages 2-15 through 2-18	pages 2-15 through 2-17

3. New or changed material is indicated by an asterisk (*).

4. File this transmittal sheet in front of the publication for reference purposes.

DISTRIBUTION RESTRICTION: Approved for public release; distribution is unlimited.

By order of the Secretary of the Army:

MARTIN E. DEMPSEY
General, United States Army
Chief of Staff

Official:

JOYCE E. MORROW
Administrative Assistant to the
Secretary of the Army
1113104

DISTRIBUTION:
Active Army, Army National Guard, and United States Army Reserve: Not to be distributed.
Electronic media only.

PCN: 144 00019100.

PIN: 100721-001

This page intentionally left blank.

Army Tactics, Techniques, and Procedures
No. 3-97.11

Marine Corps Reference Publication
No. 3-35.1D

Headquarters
Department of the Army
Washington, DC

Headquarters
Marine Corps Combat Development Command
Department of the Navy
Headquarters
United States Marine Corp

28 January 2011

Cold Region Operations

Contents

*This publication supersedes FM 31-70, dated 12 April 1968, and FM 31-71, dated 21 June 1971.

Marine Corps PCN: 14400019100

Figures

Tables

Preface

This Army tactics, techniques, and procedures (ATTP)/Marine Corps reference publication (MCRP) is the Army's doctrinal publication for operations in the cold region environment. Marines can utilize this publication as an operational reference with the 3-35 doctrinal series. It provides doctrinal guidance and direction for how United States (U.S.) forces conduct cold region operations.

The purpose of ATTP 3-97.11/MCRP 3-35.1D is to arm leaders, Soldiers, and Marines with the necessary knowledge on how to operate in cold region environments. The information contained in this manual applies to all Soldiers and Marines, regardless of rank or job specialty. This manual is designed to work with and complement field manual (FM) 3-97.6, *Mountain Operations*, and FM 3-97.61, *Military Mountaineering*. This manual will enable leaders, Soldiers, and Marines to accurately describe cold region environments, their effects on military equipment, impacts these environments have on personnel, and most importantly, how to employ the elements of combat power in cold region environments.

This ATTP provides the conceptual framework for conventional forces to conduct cold region operations within the construct of full spectrum operations, across the spectrum of conflict. It addresses cold region operations at operational and tactical levels. Chapter 1 discusses the characteristics of the cold region environment. Chapter 2 discusses the operations process. Chapter 3 identifies and discusses special considerations for operations in a cold region environment. Chapter 4 discusses how to conduct movement and maneuver in a cold region environment. Chapter 5 discusses how to apply sustainment principles unique to cold regions. Chapter 6 discusses how to apply combat power in the cold region environment. The two appendixes detail the special uniform, equipment, and heaters necessary in the cold region environment.

This publication applies to the Active Army, the Army National Guard (ARNG)/Army National Guard of the United States (ARNGUS), United States Army Reserve (USAR), Marine Corps, and Marine Corps Reserve unless otherwise stated.

Note for Marines: This manual is intended as an operational-level reference only. Some differences apply in clothing, equipment, vehicles, and aircraft (items the Marine Corps has that the Army does not and vice versa). These Marine Corps-specific differences and tactical-level differences (arising from the employment of heavy vice light infantry) are covered in MCRP 3-35.1A, *Small-Unit Leader's Guide to Cold Weather Operations*. The clothing, equipment, and tactics, techniques, and procedures for cold weather warfighting by Marines are covered in MCRP 3-35.1B, *Instructor's Guide to Combat Skiing*. By December 2011, the Marine Corps will update these publications and change the titles. The United States Marine Corps (USMC) lead agency and doctrinal proponent for mountain and cold region operations is the Marine Corps Mountain Warfare Training Center (MCMWTC) in Bridgeport, California. Contact MCMWTC, Operations and Training for further information.

The proponent of this publication is the United States Army Training and Doctrine Command (TRADOC). The preparing agency is the Combined Arms Doctrine Directorate, U.S. Army Combined Arms Center. Send written comments and recommendations on Department of the Army (DA) Form 2028 (Recommended Changes to Publications and Blank Forms) directly to: Commander, U.S. Army Combined Arms Center and Fort Leavenworth, ATTN: ATZL-MCK-D (ATTP 3-97.11), 300 McPherson Avenue (Building 463), Fort Leavenworth, KS 66027-1352. Send comments and recommendations by e-mail to leav-cadd-web-cadd@conus.army.mil. Follow the DA Form 2028 format or submit an electronic DA Form 2028.

Introduction

When conducting military operations in cold regions, leaders, Soldiers, and Marines must plan to fight two enemies: the cold and the opposing force. Despite the difficulties that cold regions pose, there are armies that have prepared for and can conduct large-scale, sustained operations in cold environments. In contrast, few U.S. Army units or personnel have trained extensively in cold region operations. Since the events of 9-11 and the shift of focus from Cold War threats, much institutional knowledge has been lost on how to operate in cold regions effectively. Some of this knowledge resides in units and individual Soldiers and Marines who have fought in Bosnia and Afghanistan, but experienced Soldiers and Marines need to present these lessons to the whole force so every Soldier and Marine can take advantage of them. For those trained in how to operate in cold region environments effectively, they will not only survive but prosper when they use their training as a combat multiplier. This has been proven repeatedly in history. In the year 1200, Norwegians used skis to enhance movement and maneuver. In 1941, the Russians—nearly defeated in the summer of that year—held the line before Leningrad and Moscow until winter and finally turned the German offense to the south. In World War II, the U.S. Army suffered 84,000 casualties due to the cold.

Cold regions can be extremely intimidating. Despite this, leaders, Soldiers, and Marines can fight and win in cold regions. As always, the keys are preparation and training. Preparation includes understanding the environment and its effects on Soldiers, Marines, and equipment and ensuring that U.S. forces have the proper clothing and equipment to accomplish their tasks. Although the Army's equipment is among the best in the world for use in cold regions, training must include knowing how to use that equipment and how to adapt operations. Cold regions also present unique challenges for the sustainment forces. Realistic and challenging training can prepare leaders, Soldiers, and Marines for the rigors of cold region warfare, allowing them the opportunity to develop the discipline and confidence that operating in the cold demands.

While Soldiers and Marines can train on some base skills and knowledge in the classroom or through self-study, experiential-based training in the terrain and weather are the only way to develop the skill set required to operate successfully. Cold regions place high demands upon leaders, Soldiers, and equipment. It requires the use of specialized clothing (see chapter 3), equipment (see chapters 4 and 5), and procedures (see chapter 2) to combat the effects of cold. Units develop robust training programs to prepare Soldiers and Marines for this environment. Depending on the time available for units to prepare, the Army's Northern Warfare Training Center located in Fort Wainwright, Alaska has developed a baseline training program for cold regions. This Cold Weather Orientation Course helps prepare Soldiers for operations in the cold region environment. This course is a baseline program only. Units need to develop additional training that applies cold region environment skills and knowledge to specific job tasks and/or to achieve proficiency in other mission essential tasks. Marines train at the Marine Corps Mountain Warfare Training Center (MCMWTC) in Bridgeport, California for individual and collective training in both cold weather and mountain warfare. Both Soldiers and Marines can train at any location. Both Soldiers and Marines should use ATTP 3-97.11D/MCRP 3-35.1D in conjunction with FM 3-97.6, *Mountain Operations*.

This page intentionally left blank.

Chapter 1
Definition and Characteristics of Cold Regions

The severe environmental conditions associated with the cold regions can render individuals and units combat ineffective without ever engaging the enemy. As energy resources dwindle, development in resource rich cold regions will increase the probability of conflicts in this environment. This chapter provides leaders, Soldiers, and Marines with cold region terrain and weather characteristics that impact military operations.

DEFINING COLD REGIONS

1-1. For military purposes, cold regions are defined as any region where cold temperatures, unique terrain, and snowfall significantly affect military operations for one month or more each year. About one quarter of the earth's land mass may be termed severely cold. In figure 1-1, this area is indicated by the area above line A in the Northern Hemisphere and below line A in the Southern Hemisphere. In these areas, mean annual air temperatures stay below freezing, maximum snow depths exceed 60 centimeters, and ice covers lakes and rivers for more than 180 days each year. Another quarter of the earth is termed moderately cold. In figure 1-1, this area fits between lines A and B (including most of the United States and Eurasia). Its mean temperatures during the coldest month are below freezing.

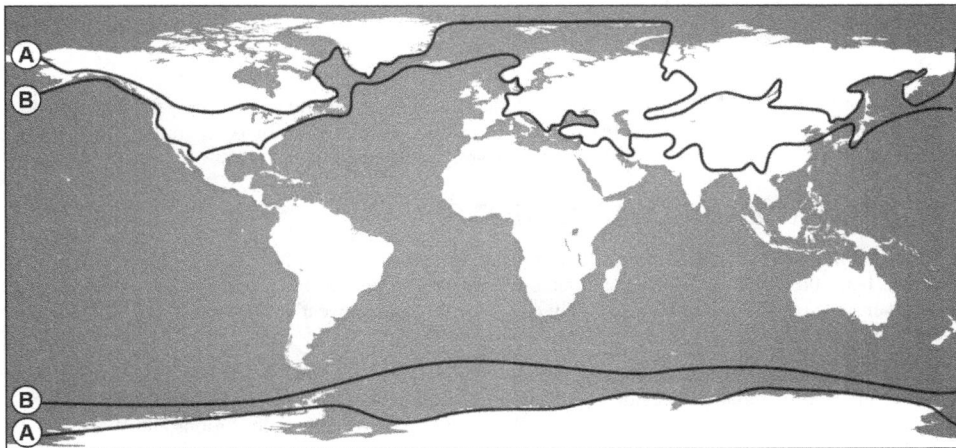

Figure 1-1. Cold regions of the world

1-2. Military forces use more than one classification system to break down cold regions into subregions. This discussion is loosely derived from the Bailey's ecoregions geographical classification system (see AR 70-38 for more detailed information). Cold regions are further broken down into the arctic, subarctic, and temperate subregions. These are simplifications of biomes; this classification system considers climate, latitude, and terrain features recognizable across the globe. All three subregions can include mountains, which significantly complicate operations in cold regions. All mountain areas that receive snowfall are considered cold regions.

ARCTIC REGION

1-3. The southern limit of the Arctic military operating environment is located at the Arctic Circle (latitude 66° 32' N). Above this latitude, the sun never sets on the summer solstice, and the sun never rises during the winter solstice. Located in the northern continental fringes of North America, Iceland, coastal Greenland, and the Arctic coast of Eurasia, this military operating environment has long, severe winters and short, cool summers. The mean monthly temperature of the warmest month hovers between 32 °F and 50 °F (0 °C and 10 °C). Annual precipitation is less than 8 inches (200 millimeters), but low rates of evaporation make the climate humid. Vegetation consists of low-growing grasses, lichens, mosses, and brush with treeless plains. Soils are poorly developed and have a permanently frozen sub-layer (permafrost) that may seasonally thaw at the surface. Surface and subsurface drainage is poor creating muddy summertime conditions. The Arctic predominately consists of coastal plains, low-interior and high-interior plains, and lesser areas of low and high-relief mountains. Most development and infrastructure of military interest centers around ports and areas with valuable natural resources (such as soil and natural gas). Few roads or towns exist.

SUBARCTIC REGION

1-4. The subarctic is the area between latitude 50° N and the Arctic Circle. At least one month of the year has a mean monthly temperature above 50 °F (10 °C). Precipitation falls mostly in the summer months. Vegetation consists primarily of needle-leaf forests and open woodlands. Soils are acidic, seasonally frozen, and contain discontinuous permafrost. Numerous lakes, ponds, peat bogs, and swamps exist because of poor subsurface drainage. The subarctic consists of coastal plains, high-relief and low-relief mountains, lesser areas of low-interior and high-interior plains, and extensive areas of rock and non-cohesive sand. There is typically more infrastructure and developed areas than in the arctic military operating environments, but vast undeveloped areas with few roads dominate. The largest temperature range in the world exists here. Snow cover exists for at least 6 months in the lowlands; surrounding mountains can have perennial snow cover.

TEMPERATE REGION

1-5. Temperate areas vary greatly and include maritime and continental zones, heavily forested areas, mountain ranges, deserts, and plains areas. The effects of cold on military operations in this region are generally short term, but these effects can be catastrophic for unprepared units.

MOUNTAINS AND COLD REGIONS

1-6. Variations in climate that exist within cold regions often result from mountainous terrain. Figure 1-2 (page 1-3) illustrates the world's mountain zones. Mountain terrain usually causes vertical changes in weather called zonations and occasionally causes differences in weather on the windward and leeward side of the mountains.

1-7. Mountains can significantly complicate operations in cold regions. Leaders should treat all mountains and mountainous regions that receive a predictable amount of snowfall as a cold region. Many tasks needed to operate successfully in cold regions apply to mountain regions; however, operating in mountainous terrain requires specialized training beyond the scope of this manual. Factors such as slope, soil composition, and surface configuration differentiates mountain operations from other cold region operations. The most significant factor to affect individual performance is altitude. Performance starts to degrade after personnel ascend to elevations over 5,000 feet (1,500 meters). Refer to FM 3-97.6 and FM 3-97.61 for more specific information.

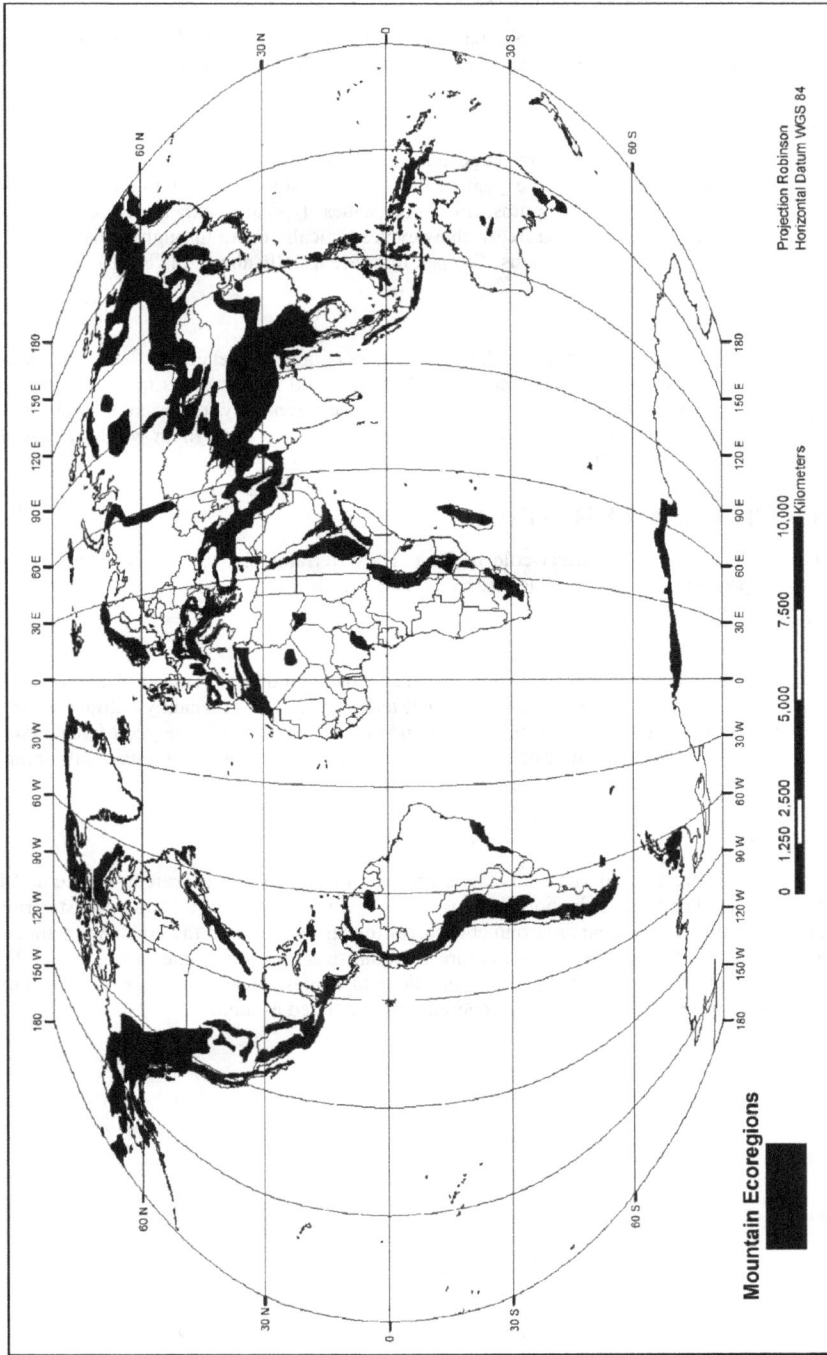

Figure 1-2. Mountain regions of the world

INFLUENCE OF OCEANS AND LAND MASSES

1-8. In addition to the influence of mountain regions on climate, large bodies of water (maritime zones) and inland areas (continental zones) have the greatest overall effect on the climate of an area.

MARITIME ZONE

1-9. A maritime zone is influenced by large bodies of water, be it an ocean or large lake. It typically moderates temperatures throughout the year with cool, wet summers and milder winters with heavy precipitation. During the winter months, maritime zones typically experience cold-wet conditions. Temperatures hover near freezing, and freeze-thaw cycles typically occur throughout the winter. Wet snow, sleet, and rain are also common conditions. Temperatures are usually above 14 °F (-10 °C).

CONTINENTAL ZONES

1-10. Continental zones are inland areas; the climate is generally influenced by large land masses. These zones typically remain drier than maritime zones. Extreme cold temperatures in winter and warm to hot temperatures in summer are the norm. Continental zones generally experience cold-dry conditions. Temperatures stay below 14 °F (-10 °C), the ground remains frozen throughout winter, freeze-thaw cycles rarely occur and the snow is light and dry.

TERRAIN CHARACTERISTICS

1-11. Characteristics of terrain affect cold regions. These terrains characteristics include icecaps, boreal forests, tundra, permafrost, muskeg, glaciers, rivers, and overflow ice.

ICECAPS

1-12. The icecap includes the large ice sheets—such as those found in Greenland, Antarctica, and on small islands—in the high northern latitudes. Mean annual temperatures are constantly below freezing, with low amounts of annual precipitation occurring as snow and landscapes generally devoid of vegetation and soils. Most development and infrastructure of military interest centers on ports and areas with valuable natural resources (such as oil and natural gas). Few roads or towns exist.

BOREAL FORESTS

1-13. Thick boreal forests, also known as taiga, are vast areas in which evergreen spruce and firs are the dominant plant life. The taiga is the northernmost area where trees can exist. Boreal forests grow primarily in the subarctic military operating environment; boreal forests can grow in the arctic and temperate regions as well (see figure 1-3). The extent of these forests diminishes the further one moves north. The tree line (with respect to elevation) is generally low. Transitions to treeless areas can occur at elevations as low as 2,000 feet (610 meters). Treeless areas are generally characterized as tundra.

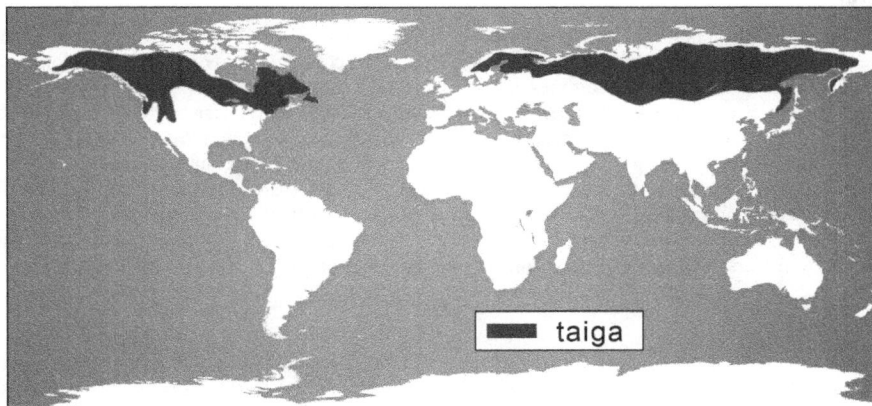

Figure 1-3. Extent of boreal forests (taiga)

TUNDRA

1-14. The tundra is an area where tree growth is hindered due to low temperatures and a short growing season. Tundra is the most prevalent terrain feature north of the subarctic. Tundra consists of various grasses and mosses. Vegetation often develops into clumps with standing pools of water between clumps—called tussocks—and make mounted and dismounted movement extremely difficult during the summer and during freeze-thaw periods. The tundra has been known to swallow vehicles as they sink into the swampy ground. Movement is easier in the winter when the ground is frozen. Even with the frozen ground of winter, vehicular movement is generally restricted to roads. Movement on tundra can quickly turn into a vehicle recovery operation. Drainage in these areas is typically poor due to the permanently frozen ground that exists under the tundra. This is known as permafrost.

PERMAFROST

1-15. Permafrost is permanently frozen ground that occurs when the ground temperature is 32 °F (0 °C) or colder for two or more years. It is continuous in the arctic military operating environments but sporadic in the subarctic and nonexistent in temperate regions. The thickness of permafrost varies from a few feet to over a thousand feet in depth. Disturbance of the tundra increases the thawing of permafrost. In areas where permafrost is present, Soldiers and Marines will build fighting positions above ground unless they have engineer support. Frozen ground prevents the draining of water, contributing to the formation of muskeg.

MUSKEG

1-16. Muskeg is a type of bog or wetland found in poorly drained areas underlain with permafrost. Muskeg develops in areas with abundant rainfall and cool summers. Trapped by underlying permafrost, water moves little or not at all. Acid from slowly rotting plants accumulates in stagnant water and lowers soil pH. Due to the acidic soil, only a few specialized plants grow in this environment. Personnel can quickly spot this terrain when black spruce (mainly in the subarctic), sphagnum moss, and sedges grow in abundance. Muskeg can hinder or facilitate mobility depending on the season and temperature. Sedges replace grasses, which prefer warmer, dryer conditions. Usually the ground is soft and spongy, but it can be a vast shallow swamp. Again, movement is difficult in the summer but gets easier in the winter when the ground is frozen. These areas often prove difficult to detect in early or late winter when the ground is only partially frozen. Vehicles that attempt to move through muskegs at this time often get trapped.

GLACIERS

1-17. Glaciers are rivers of ice and snow that develop with the seasonal accumulation of snow in valleys where the summer temperature stays low enough to prevent complete snow melt. The accumulated snow eventually turns to ice through compression forces. Gravity causes the flow or movement of glaciers; glaciers glide over a layer of melt-water between the underside of the glacier and the surface of the earth. Glaciers and polar icecaps cover 10 percent of the earth's surface, of which Alaska contains 2 percent of the total glaciers. Typically, glaciers occur in mountainous regions of the subarctic and temperate zones. Glaciers are the highway into the mountains, normally being easier and safer to negotiate than the surrounding ridges and peaks. However, glaciers can prove exceedingly dangerous if Soldiers and Marines fail to familiarize themselves with the unique terrain. Soldiers and Marines require specialized training and equipment to traverse and negotiate over and around crevasses and ice falls.

RIVERS

1-18. Rivers found in cold regions may aid movements or be major obstacles depending on the time of year and mission. Subarctic rivers are usually glacier-fed with many braided channels and swift currents. Glacier-fed rivers change course frequently, making river navigation difficult and rendering map data suspect. If units have shallow-draught boats available, rivers may provide valuable lines of communication in summer. Once firmly frozen, rivers may offer routes for both mounted and dismounted movement. During spring and early winter (when the rivers experience break-up and freeze-up), rivers often become impassable. Some rivers, especially in temperate areas, may not freeze solidly enough to allow for winter movement.

OVERFLOW ICE

1-19. Overflow ice occurs when a layer of ice ruptures and water underneath it flows up through the surface. Two conditions must exist for overflow ice to occur. First, temperatures must be below freezing. As a water source freezes, it does so from the top down. Second, subsurface water must be under pressure. If the water under the layer of ice is under pressure (for example where a spring continues to flow into the area), the water can force its way through ice and flow on top of it. Overflow ice can occur throughout the winter despite extremely cold temperatures. Ice can rupture and re-freeze many times, forming layer upon layer of ice. Overflow ice can be difficult to detect and can create a significant obstacle along roadways. Despite extremely cold temperatures, men and equipment may become immersed in water. Aufeis is ice that has built up as a result of overflow throughout the winter; it can persist on rivers well into the summer months and presents another obstacle to movement on rivers that are otherwise ice free.

TERRAIN ANALYSIS

1-20. As in all tactical operations, terrain analysis involves observation and fields of fire, avenues of approach, key terrain, obstacles, cover and concealment (known as OAKOC). For the Marine Corps, it involves key terrain, observation, and fields of fire, cover and concealment, obstacles, and avenues of approach (known as KOCOA). Successful cold region operations require that commanders and staffs understand the terrain characteristics and hazards.

OBSERVATION AND FIELDS OF FIRE

1-21. In the arctic and subarctic military operating environments, conditions often resemble desert regions with respect to observation and fields of fire. Generally, the terrain is open with little high vegetation and allows for unrestricted visibility though there is still complex terrain. In areas with boreal forests (see paragraph 1-13), visibility becomes extremely limited, especially in old growth spruce and fir forests. This condition is limited in the arctic military operating environment but extensive in the subarctic military operating environment. Snow and light conditions also greatly impact observation and fields of fire. Winds can create ground blizzards, restricting operations for long periods. Long periods of darkness and twilight can further restrict observation. Whiteouts and grayouts also hinder visibility. Conversely, moonlit nights over snow-covered terrain can provide relatively good observation and fields of fire. The looming phenomena in extreme cold conditions can make range estimation difficult. Featureless tundra can create the same effect in the summer and winter. Long periods of daylight in the summer months reduce or eliminate the option of conducting operations under limited visibility.

AVENUES OF APPROACH

1-22. Avenues of approach depend mainly on man-made roads and trails. When the ice is thick enough, units can use waterways cleared of snow or construct ice roads. Units can use some specialized tracked vehicles such as bulldozers to open otherwise restricted and severely restricted terrain. Soldiers and Marines properly trained and equipped with skis or snowshoes can effectively move cross-country; those without the equipment or training will need to remain close to roads and trails. Units can use river networks to move personnel and supplies quickly over long distances in the summer months.

KEY TERRAIN

1-23. The most important terrain features in the cold regions are major road networks (lines of communications) and any developed or urban areas. For small units, shelter adds to combat effectiveness. Increased logistics requirements necessitate access to developed areas on a larger scale than most planners anticipate. In extreme cold regions, battles to control this key terrain are common. Passes, the high ground that can control a key pass, and river networks are also key terrain.

OBSTACLES

1-24. Snow and ice present obvious challenges to wheeled, tracked, and individual. (See chapter 4). Often, units require extensive engineer efforts to keep roads open. Combat engineers may prove the most valuable and necessary resource for large-scale military operations conducted in cold regions. Lack of roads often require units to construct roads and trails. Limited frost-free days make this a time-consuming and difficult prospect. Other options used to overcome these obstacles include constructing ice roads and winter trails or using frozen waterways. Chinook winds that bring a thaw can temporarily bring military operations to a halt as roads flood and turn to impassable mud. The break-up period in spring can also slow military operations to a crawl. For cross-country movement, snow presents a significant obstacle to Soldiers and Marines not trained in the use of skis or snowshoes. Cross-country movement during the summer months is equally difficult. Thick forests, swampy tundra, and muskeg restrict vehicle movement to roads and trails. Off road, individuals move in a slow and arduous manner.

COVER AND CONCEALMENT

1-25. Intervisibility lines may provide the only means of cover or concealment in the arctic and subarctic military operating environments. In the boreal forests, concealment is excellent. Small diameter spruce and fir trees provide limited cover from small arms fire; under indirect fires, these small trees will create additional flying debris. Where the ground is frozen, personnel can use snow and ice to create effective fighting positions.

WEATHER CHARACTERISTICS

1-26. Weather characteristics in the cold region environment consist of the type of cold, snowfall, and unique phenomena.

COLD TEMPERATURE CATEGORIES

1-27. The Army and Marine Corps group cold temperatures using the same categories. However, the Army is designed to operate in colder temperatures than the Marine Corps. Considering this, the Army adds an extra category. The temperature categories are—
- Wet cold: +39 °F to +20 °F (4 °C to -6 °C).
- Dry cold: +19 °F to -4 °F (-7 °C to -20 °C).
- Intense cold: -5 °F to -25 °F (-20 °C to -32 °C).

- Extreme cold: -25 °F to -40 °F (-32 °C to -40 °C).
- (Army only) hazardous cold: -40 °F (-40 °C) and below.

1-28. Wet cold conditions occur when wet snow and rain often accompany wet cold conditions. This type of environment is often more dangerous to troops and equipment than the colder, dry cold environments because the ground becomes slushy and muddy, and clothing and equipment becomes perpetually wet and damp. Because water conducts heat 25 times faster than air, core body temperatures can quickly drop if troops become wet and then caught in a blowing wind. Troops can rapidly become casualties due to weather if not properly equipped, trained, and led. Wet cold environments combined with wind can be even more dangerous because of the wind's effect on the body's perceived temperature. Wet cold can quickly lead to hypothermia, frost bite, and trench foot. Wet cold conditions exist not only in mountain environments but in many other environments during seasonal transition periods. Under wet cold conditions, the ground alternates between freezing and thawing because the temperatures fluctuate above and below the freezing point. This makes planning problematic. For example, areas that are trafficable when frozen could become severely restricted if the ground thaws.

1-29. Dry cold conditions are easier to live in than wet cold conditions. Like wet cold, proper equipment, training, and leadership are critical to successful operations. Wind chill is a complicating factor in this type of cold. Of the four cold weather categories, the dry cold environment best enables troops to survive because of low humidity and the permanently frozen ground. As a result, people and equipment are not subject to the effects of the thawing and freezing cycle, and precipitation is generally in the form of dry snow.

1-30. Intense cold exists from -5 °F to -25 °F (-20 °C to -32 °C) and can affect the mind as much as the body. Intense cold has a rapid numbing effect. Simple tasks take longer and require more effort than in warmer temperatures, and the quality of work degrades as attention-to-detail diminishes. Clothing becomes more bulky to compensate for the cold so troops lose dexterity. Commanders must consider these factors when planning operations and assigning tasks.

1-31. Extreme cold occurs when temperatures fall below -25 °F (-32 °C), and the challenge of survival becomes paramount. During extreme cold conditions, individuals can easily prioritize physical comfort above all else. Personnel may withdraw into themselves and adopt a cocoon-like existence. Leaders must expect and plan for weapons, vehicles, and munitions failures in this environment. As in other categories, leadership, training, and specialized equipment is critical to the ability to operate successfully.

1-32. In hazardous cold conditions, commanders and planners assume a great deal of risk if they choose to engage in operations when the temperature falls below -40 °F (-40 °C). Units must have extensive training before undertaking an operation in these temperature extremes.

SNOW CATEGORIES

1-33. For military purposes, snow is categorized as light, moderate, or heavy. Each classification affects visibility and ground movement due to accumulation:

- Light snow-visibility is equal to or greater than 5/8 mile (or 1,000 meters) in falling snow. A trace to 1 inch (2.5 centimeters) per hour accumulates.
- Moderate snow-visibility is 5/16 mile to half a statute mile (or 500–900 meters) in falling snow. One to three inches (2.5 to 7.6 centimeters) per hour accumulates.
- Heavy snow-visibility is cut to less than 1/4 statute miles (or 400 meters) in falling snow. Three or more inches per hour accumulates.

1-34. Units can use snow and snowdrifts to their advantage on the battlefield. Snow fills in ditches and vehicle tracks. On rolling ground, snow tends to flatten the terrain. The wind builds up snowdrifts and can change the contour of the ground a great deal. Troops must continually study snow-covered terrain and utilize every feature. On the downwind side of every obstacle, tree, house, and bush, a hollow always exists. This hollow provides an excellent observation point or firing position. The wind, particularly in open areas, may form long, wavy snowdrifts that create almost natural snow trenches. When deep enough, Soldiers and Marines can use them as an approach to the objective.

1-35. Units can use frozen streams or sunken riverbeds as another means of advance. Often they may represent a longer but safer route. However, leaders still consider overflow ice (see paragraph 1-19). If the ice is not thick enough, units will quickly find themselves immobilized. Soldiers and Marines must consider that certain swampy areas do not freeze solidly during the coldest periods of winter. Often, these swampy areas are covered with snow, hiding the water underneath and making the swamps an obstacle. Only experience and the knowledge that swamps exist in the local area will prevent accidents. Soldiers and Marines should avoid and bypass suspected areas without attempting to cross.

WEATHER PHENOMENA

1-36. Weather information can be hard to come by in cold regions. Observatories make generalized forecasts for large, unpopulated areas that may or may not be accurate. A call for moderate weather conditions in the forecast may not be relevant to the particular area of operations, and local conditions may overwhelm unprepared forces. For specific information on weather observation and forecasting, refer to FM 3-97.61. Unique weather phenomena can affect military operations in cold region environments:

- Ice fog.
- Blizzard.
- Whiteout.
- Grayout.
- Temperature inversion.
- Looming.
- Chinook winds.
- Aurora borealis.
- Light data.

ICE FOG

1-37. Ice fog occurs when three things exist: temperature of -30 °F (-34 °C) or colder, a vapor source, and still air conditions. Moisture from heat sources that use combustion crystallize in the air forming a fog of very small ice particles. Firing a weapon creates heat. The resulting ice fog pinpoints the weapon's position with a lasting signature. Soldiers and Marines require alternate firing positions for both target acquisition and cover and concealment. Stationary running vehicles can also produce ice fog creating a signature around them noticeable for miles.

BLIZZARD

1-38. A blizzard consists of the following conditions for three or more hours:

- Sustained winds or frequent gusts to 35 miles (56 kilometers) per hour or greater.
- Considerable falling, blowing, or falling and blowing snow.
- Reduced visibility to a quarter-mile or less.

Ground blizzards involve winds moving snow already on the ground. This hazard often occurs in the arctic and subarctic. This phenomenon can last for days.

WHITEOUT

1-39. A whiteout occurs when sunlight is diffused through an unbroken cloud layer onto an unbroken snow surface. The horizon effectively disappears. Individuals experience a loss of depth perception and an inability to distinguish irregularities in terrain. Whiteout, often referred to as flat light, creates difficult and dangerous travel. Units should restrict or cease movement until the condition clears.

GRAYOUT

1-40. A grayout occurs over a snow-covered surface during twilight or when the sun is close to the horizon. It results in an overall grayness to surroundings causing a loss of depth perception. During grayout, the horizon is indistinguishable making travel difficult and dangerous.

TEMPERATURE INVERSIONS

1-41. Normally as elevation increases, temperature decreases. In mountainous areas, the general rule is for every 1,000 feet of elevation gained, the temperature decreases 3 °F to 5 °F. When cold, calm, clear conditions exist, temperature inversions are the exception to this rule. During a troop movement or climb started in a valley, troops often encounter higher temperatures as they gain altitude. This reversal of normal cooling with elevation is called a temperature inversion. Temperature inversions occur when snow, ice, and heat loss through thermal radiation cool the mountain air. The cooler air settles into valleys and low areas. The inversion continues until the sun warms the surface of the earth or a moderate wind causes a mixing of the warm and cold air layers. Temperatures can differ by as much as 20 degrees warmer on hills or mountainsides that are just a few hundred feet from the valley floor.

LOOMING

1-42. Looming is an optical illusion. Objects appear closer and taller than they actually are. This condition exists in cold still air and can make range estimation inaccurate.

CHINOOK WINDS

1-43. Chinook winds are warm, dry winds that occur in the lee of high mountain ranges. In a few short hours, these winds can produce complete thaws in cold regions that typically do not see a thaw until the spring or summer months. Such conditions mimic the spring break-up period typical of cold regions. Resulting mud and flooding on roads and trails may make them impassable. Frozen rivers and lakes may partially thaw making them unreliable as transportation routes.

AURORA BOREALIS

1-44. The aurora borealis is caused by charged particles produced by the sun, deflected by the earth's magnetic field, and drawn towards the poles. These charged particles create a light show in the sky being most visible on cold clear nights. The aurora borealis occurs throughout the year. It has been reported as far south as Mexico City. It disrupts amplitude modulation communications but can enhance frequency modulation communications. In the Southern Hemisphere the aurora borealis is known as aurora australis.

LIGHT DATA

1-45. During winter, especially in the arctic and subarctic, night operations are the norm. On clear, cold, windless, moonlit nights, personnel can see exceptionally well over open snow-covered terrain. During the winter months, twilight provides some visibility even though the sun has set. However, in a snow-covered forest (taiga), it becomes extremely dark.

1-46. Sunrise, sunset, and the amount of useable light available for operations becomes relative to where Soldiers are physically located. Leaders, Soldiers, and Marines may use the information contained in figure 1-4 to approximate the number of daylight hours available for a given part of the year. Light data depends on latitude and time of year. Soldiers and Marines should realize that sunrise and sunset times swing dramatically in the arctic and subarctic. For example, as the seasons change into spring and summer in Anchorage, Alaska, each day grows approximately 6 minutes longer. This effect reverses itself after the summer solstice. At its most extreme, 24 hours of darkness or 24 hours of light occur, depending on the time of year.

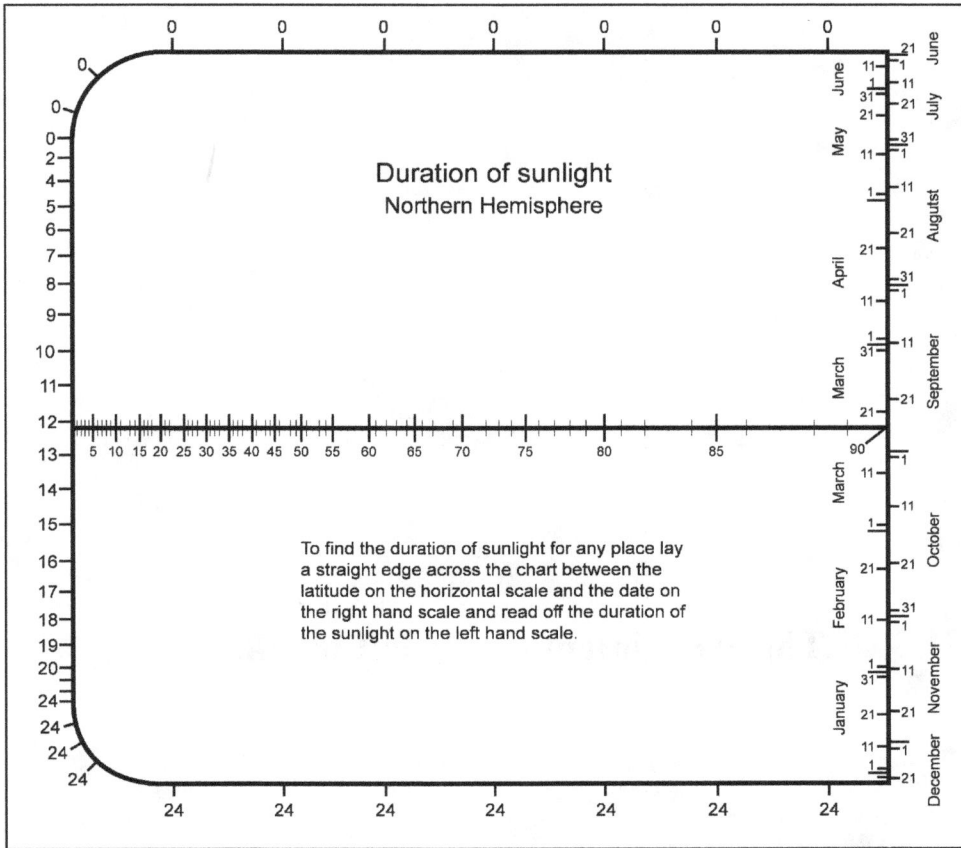

Figure 1-4. Daylight chart

This page intentionally left blank.

Chapter 2

Conducting Full Spectrum Operations in Cold Regions

The Army's operational concept is full spectrum operations. Army forces combine offensive, defensive, and stability or civil support operations simultaneously to seize, retain, and exploit the initiative. These forces accept prudent risk to create opportunities to achieve decisive results. This chapter discusses how military forces conduct full spectrum operations in cold regions.

OFFENSIVE OPERATIONS

2-1. *Offensive operations* are combat operations conducted to defeat and destroy enemy forces and seize terrain, resources, and population centers. They impose the commander's will on the enemy (FM 3-0). Marines conduct operations to take the initiative from the enemy, gain freedom of action, and mass effects to achieve objectives. The four types of offensive operations are movement to contact, attack, exploitation, and pursuit. Offense is the decisive element in full spectrum operations and preferred posture of the Army during conflicts. These fundamental goals apply in temperate climates; however, certain aspects are emphasized when conducting offensive operations in the cold region environment. The most important element of a successful operation is the ability to maneuver to defeat or destroy the enemy. This task is challenging in cold region environments where the terrain and climate are not conducive to maneuvering.

2-2. If combat operations are decided upon during snow storms or high winds, then leaders are encouraged to keep compact formations, simple plans, detailed instructions, and limited objectives as well as to use positive means of identification. Units can conduct close reconnaissance and attack under the cover afforded by such conditions. Successful operations require that Soldiers and Marines have experience in operating in cold conditions due to the high demand it places on them. If Soldiers and Marines have little or no experience in operating in the cold region environment, then leaders should not engage in offensive operations if possible during inclement weather. If a mission needs to be undertaken, then commanders use compact formations to maximize command and control.

2-3. After seizing an objective, units attempt to consolidate and reorganize it. Assaulting troops often grow fatigued and overheated from the exertion of the attack. Leaders make provisions to prevent personnel from becoming cold or heat casualties. They integrate exploitation forces into offensive plans. Once dislodged from defensive positions, enemy forces are at the mercy of the extreme cold and difficult terrain found in cold region environments. This provides an excellent opportunity for follow-on forces to continue the offensive, exploit the enemy, and force him to surrender or be destroyed.

CHARACTERISTICS OF OFFENSIVE OPERATIONS

2-4. Special characteristics of the offense in the cold region environment apply as special considerations to warfighting functions. FM 1-02/MCRP 5-12A describes the characteristics of offensive operations as surprise, concentration, tempo, and audacity. The cold region environment presents unique opportunities and challenges with each of these characteristics.

Surprise

2-5. Local surprise may be more difficult to achieve when snow is present. The enemy can easily see moving objects on the snow and hear Soldiers and Marines moving because of better sound transmission in cold air. Additionally, the enemy may occupy specific locations so that the only way surprise can be obtained is by limited visibility. If ample over-snow transportation exists, suddenly increasing the tempo of an initially slow attack through the snow may surprise the enemy.

2-6. Commanders make all efforts to execute assaults at night or during periods of low visibility. However, they may not be able to capitalize on periods of darkness or visibility in the arctic and subarctic depending on the time of year. Considering the importance of surprise, it may be preferable to deliver the assault without field artillery preparation fires.

Concentration

2-7. Units must concentrate overwhelming combat power at critical points of the attack. In cold regions, concentration of forces may prove extremely difficult due to mobility restrictions and periods of limited visibility. Therefore, all units must be equipped, trained, and experienced in moving under such conditions.

Tempo

2-8. *Tempo* is the relative speed and rhythm of military operations over time with respect to the enemy (FM 3-0). Units build it by carefully planning for the avenue of attack, the battle in depth, a quick transition to other phases of the offense, and the concentration of forces. In cold regions, key planning factors for this include time, speed, and mobility. Planners need additional time for troop leading procedures and preparation for combat. They need speed and mobility for tactical movement by forward troops and the reserve forces. Additional lead time may be required for initiating reconnaissance. The sustainment effort may need to be augmented by techniques—such as prepositioning forward or using aircraft for resupply— to maintain the offensive tempo.

Audacity

2-9. Effectively using weather conditions increases opportunities for audacity in conducting attacks. This includes exploiting blizzards, falling snow, fog, low cloud cover, and natural night illumination. Leaders can imaginatively use what appear to be weather obstacles and turn them into major advantages. However, conducting offensive operations during severe weather conditions restricts the use of aviation support, increases reconnaissance problems (such as sensor degradation), and may reduce the length of reconnaissance patrols. Commanders weigh this advantage against losing command and control of their units. They use detailed plans to mitigate this risk. If commanders decide to attack during blizzards or a blowing snow storm, the unit should attack downwind or at a slight angle to force the enemy to face the full force of the storm.

TYPES OF OFFENSIVE OPERATIONS

2-10. Leaders employ the same basic four types of offensive tasks as they do in more temperate regions. However, they emphasize the ability to easily transition between movement to contact, attack, exploitation, and pursuit to capitalize on the gains that units achieve in the offense.

Movement to Contact

2-11. To gain or reestablish contact with the enemy, units conduct a movement to contact. As mobility decreases, units use a smaller force to establish contact. If mobility conditions vary because of differences in snow depth or mud conditions, commanders can adjust the location for deployment into attack formation. Search and attack operations by elements skilled in cold region operations may help deny large areas to the enemy and collect information. Before a meeting engagement takes place, commanders consider their options for subsequent actions. If a unit anticipates a hasty or deliberate attack, it proceeds on multiple avenues or at reduced intervals to facilitate their rapid employment. If a unit anticipates a hasty defense, it pushes supplies immediately (such as construction materials, heaters, and additional ammunition) to the forward troops.

Attack

2-12. As the temperature drops, terrain-oriented objectives become more likely than force-oriented objectives since mobility worsens and the enemy seeks sheltered defensive positions. Units significantly impair the enemy's will and unit cohesion if they coordinate their attack as an operation in depth. Units can disrupt the enemy's ability for sustainment in cold regions by attacking lines of communications or support facilities.

2-13. Larger formations may task organize as a contingency force for hasty attack by identifying more mobile elements for maneuver tasks and rehearsing the conduct of the hasty attack. A hasty counterattack in the defense may be vital to retaining shelter from the elements and capitalizing on the enemy's fatigue before the enemy completely consolidates and reorganizes.

2-14. Commanders plan deliberate attacks, employing every available asset against the enemy defense, with an assessment of the enemy's ability to prepare a cold region defense. Although the enemy's defense may be more concentrated due to requirements for shelter and individual sustainability, this may be offset by maneuver limitations on the attacker as well as degradation of fire support assets. If the enemy's proficiency at preparing a cold region defense exceeds the friendly forces' proficiency at conducting an attack, delays in preparing for a deliberate attack may favor the enemy.

2-15. A key element in planning for counterattacks is preparation of the terrain for mobility. This may include snow removal or snow packing operations to prepare assembly areas and lanes for the counterattacking force; rehearsals help confirm movement times and actions on contact. Raids during cold weather take advantage of the enemy's reduced mobility and may be an economical means of neutralizing key support or command and control facilities.

Exploitation

2-16. Units immediately follow successful attacks by exploitation to deny the enemy sufficient time to regain the initiative. Although the forces leading the attack may continue into the exploitation, these forces may need to be rested or sheltered, and the follow-on forces may need to pass through to conduct the exploitation.

Pursuit

2-17. Transitioning from the attack or exploitation into the pursuit of a retreating enemy may take place at a point when the attacking forces are nearing the end of their endurance. Commanders temper audacity with good judgment if the cold weather presents a significant risk for injury on a broad scale. Conversely, if friendly forces can sustain a pursuit in cold regions, the combined effects of combat and the environment may annihilate the enemy.

FORMS OF MANEUVER

2-18. The forms of maneuver complement the offensive tasks and are oriented on the enemy rather than on the terrain. Reconnaissance elements provide the commander with combat information and combat intelligence as to the enemy situation, from which the commander maneuvers the friendly forces.

Envelopment

2-19. Envelopment and encirclement may become more feasible if the enemy's mobility is severely limited forcing the enemy to sacrifice flank, forward, or rear security in the interest of speed. The enemy also may neglect these security measures if road bound and lacking over-snow mobility for flank security. This may happen as the enemy conducts a movement to contact or during friendly exploitation or pursuit.

Turning Movement

2-20. Cold region operations can present great opportunities to secure key terrain. Such opportunities can hamper the enemy's ability to conduct sustainment operations, strangling the enemy's forward deployed forces and forcing them into action or to surrender. However, leaders must take care to adequately sustain friendly forces conducting this maneuver to prevent their own loss.

Infiltration

2-21. Infiltration may be particularly useful during cold weather. This especially applies if the enemy has a large defensive area and if inclement weather impairs enemy counterreconnaissance and surveillance assets. Highly mobile units, such as ski-mobile personnel or units equipped with over-snow vehicles, may be used against deeper objectives while larger, less mobile units attack more immediate key objectives.

Penetration

2-22. Units use penetration if they have poor mobility and the enemy's defense is keyed at specific points along mobility corridors.

Frontal Attack

2-23. Units can use a frontal attack across a wide front and with overwhelming superiority against a dispersed or disorganized enemy force. In an otherwise unfavorable situation, a sudden worsening of weather conditions such as a blizzard may make a frontal assault possible for well-prepared friendly forces.

Flanking Attack (USMC)

2-24. The Marine Corps has a sixth form of maneuver. A flanking attack is a form of offensive maneuver directed at the flank of an enemy force. A flank is the right or left side of a military formation and is not oriented toward the enemy. The attacker creates a flank by using fires or a successful penetration. It resembles envelopment except units conduct it on a shallower axis.

TACTICAL CONSIDERATIONS

2-25. Conducting offensive operations in cold region environments demands special techniques for reconnaissance and surveillance, camouflage, target engagement, and deception. These special techniques are developed out of necessity because of the equipment and uniforms used in this environment.

2-26. Special techniques are required to construct fighting positions in snow. In general, to construct fighting positions above ground proves more efficient due to the permafrost. However, the time of year and amount of permafrost present determine the type of fighting position to construct and the degree to which it is located above ground or below ground. FM 5-103 describes the proper method for constructing cold region environment fighting positions.

PATROL BASE OPERATIONS

2-27. Leaders have unique considerations when planning for small units to occupy patrol bases in cold region environments for resupply and rest. While some differences exist, many of the same patrol base principles apply that are used in more temperate regions. Soldiers refer to FM 3-21.8 and use that publication with the techniques found in the Army's "Cold Weather (Cold Weather Leaders Course [CWLC], Cold Weather Orientation Course [CWOC] & Arctic Light Individual Training [ALIT]) Student Handout" found on the Northern Warfare Training Center Web site. Marines refer to MCRP 3-35.1A.

Reconnaissance and Surveillance

2-28. Units operating in cold region environments are especially vulnerable to detection by using thermal devices. The winter environment significantly affects the thermal infrared signatures of targets, enhancing them unless weather conditions are degraded (such as during a snowstorm). High thermal contrasts result when low background temperatures couple with high temperatures produced by internal combustion engines, mechanical friction, and heated areas. Soldiers and Marines heat their immediate surroundings for comfort or survival. These contrasts become further enhanced when background temperatures rapidly decrease because of radiative heat loss. Poor apparent thermal contrasts exist when snow falls. The obscuring effects of snow, plus the effects of an overcast sky, may significantly reduce the target engagement ranges of infrared sensors.

2-29. A deep, undisturbed snow cover presents a relatively uniform and clutter-free background to a thermal infrared sensor if the snow is deep enough to completely cover a large area. Snow-covered areas also typically appear as the coldest element within a natural scene. These factors combine to make targets within a snow background more vulnerable to infrared detection.

2-30. Uncompacted snow emits infrared energy well but conducts heat poorly. At night, undisturbed snow surfaces cool rapidly when cloud cover suddenly decreases. This rapid cooling results since snow cannot conduct heat from the ground rapidly enough to make up for the high radiative losses at the snow surface. Objects within a snowfield will contrast with undisturbed snow under such conditions.

2-31. Patches of ground and objects, such as a log, contrast in the infrared image with the surrounding snow. Such a background creates problems for infrared guided munitions because it generates numerous potential false targets.

2-32. In winter, trees usually appear warmer than snow-covered surfaces. During the day, this occurs because trees absorb much more solar radiation than the surrounding snow. This daytime storage of heat also results in tree trunks and limbs being much warmer than the snow at night. The thermal clutter associated with a wooded area offers significant protection for an individual seeking to hide from infrared surveillance.

2-33. Soldiers and Marines are particularly vulnerable to infrared surveillance in winter because of the large difference between body temperature and a cold background. Soldiers and Marines can conceal themselves by constructing a thermal shelter. (See figure 2-1 on this page and figures 2-2 and 2-3 on page 2-6). See the "Cold Weather (Cold Weather Leaders Course [CWLC], Cold Weather Orientation Course [CWOC] & Arctic Light Individual Training [ALIT]) Student Handout" for detailed instructions on how to construct this shelter. In figure 2-2, note how the log rests outside the covered frame above the door. This simple technique works well for reconnaissance and surveillance missions since it keeps Soldiers and Marines warm while they conduct those missions. Marines refer to MCRP 3-35.1A.

Figure 2-1. Frame of infrared counterdetection (thermal) shelter

Figure 2-2. Covered frame of infrared counterdetection (thermal) shelter

Figure 2-3. Snow-covered frame of infrared counterdetection (thermal) shelter

2-34. Soldiers and Marines consider that anything mechanical (such as a stove or internal combustion engine) also makes them susceptible to detection. Camouflage nets can hide tents and heaters from visual detection, but they do little to counteract thermal detection. Snow fall provides the best security from thermal detection. Even light to moderate falling snow can neutralize thermal detection equipment. Considering this, snow storms provide ideal cover to move vehicles and troops or to launch attacks.

2-35. Leaders enforce sound discipline when conducting tactical operations in any environment. However, in the cold air, sound carries much farther than in temperate climates. U.S. forces keep all sounds to a minimum. Noise caused by motors, men coughing, and skiers breaking through snow crust may warn the enemy of activity at extreme distances.

Camouflage

2-36. Troops require special camouflage combinations in the cold region environment when snow or ice presents a white background as the prevalent feature. Soldiers and Marines who operate in cold region environments wear white covers for the upper and lower bodies, helmets, gloves, and rucksacks. See table 2-1 for the proper camouflage. See figures 2-4 and 2-5 on this page and figures 2-6 and 2-7 on page 2-8 for camouflage patterns. Marines refer to MCRP 3-35.1A.

Table 2-1. Camouflage by terrain

Terrain	Camouflage
Thick woods	Use ACU ECWCS (use over white trousers in deep snow)
Low brush or light scrub	Use over white parka and ACU ECWCS trousers
Trails and roads	Use ACU ECWCS parka and over white trousers
Above tree line and in open field	Use over whites complete
ACU Army combat uniform ECWCS Extended Cold Weather Clothing System	

Figure 2-4. Camouflage for thick woods

Figure 2-5. Camouflage for low brush or light scrub

Figure 2-6. Camouflage for trails and roads

Figure 2-7. Camouflage for above tree line and in open field

2-37. Snow exaggerates contrasts and makes camouflage essential. If time permits, Soldiers and Marines cover any tracks that reveal positions. Leaders establish deceptive track plans. Units can use snow and other natural materials to conceal trenches and foxholes by placing loose snow on the side of the enemy. U.S. forces create a gentle slope of snow for hiding all sharp angles. Leaders chose the locations of emplacements and vehicles that take advantage of existing dark patterns.

2-38. Snow banks beside plowed roads and tracks often provide excellent cover and concealment in wintertime. These banks or drifts remain far into the spring thaw period, especially in areas of heavy snowfall.

2-39. Soldiers and Marines camouflage vehicles and equipment. They paint vehicles and equipment white to blend in with the surroundings. Vehicle crews pile snow around tracks and wheels upon halting as well as follow the leader's deceptive track plan. However, Soldiers and Marines take care not to pile snow directly against the wheels or tracks. Units properly camouflage tents by scattering snow and branches on the tent after erecting it. Another technique includes taking white paper, wetting it, applying it, and allowing it to freeze on all kinds of surfaces.

2-40. At night and under other conditions of low visibility, units find it difficult to distinguish friendly forces from enemy troops when both wear white. Units require distinctive markings and signals. Markings apply not only to uniforms but to equipment.

Firing

2-41. Engaging targets in a movement to contact calls for special firing techniques in the cold region environment. These modified firing techniques are based on the individual wearing skis or snowshoes, having ski poles, and hauling an ahkio or similar sled. Each firing position has unique advantages and disadvantages. The three firing positions described in table 2-2 modify typical firing positions used in temperate regions. Marines refer to 3-35.1A. Figure 2-8 on this page and figures 2-9, 2-10, and 2-11 on page 2-10 provide additional illustrations.

Table 2-2. Cold region environment fighting positions

Position	Advantage	Disadvantage
Standing	Rapidly employ weapon system and can move on snowshoes or skis easily once firing procedures are complete	High silhouette
Kneeling	Reduced targeting profile than standing position and it is somewhat easier to stand from kneeling vs. the prone. More stability when engaging targets.	Somewhat cumbersome to come back to standing position
Prone	Low silhouette, more stability when firing weapon if snow is compacted	Cumbersome to come back to standing position from the prone since individual is wearing skis or snowshoes. The individual also has a higher risk of cold injury depending on how long they are in the snow

Figure 2-8. Standing position

Figure 2-9. Kneeling position

Figure 2-10. Prone position

Figure 2-11. Platform-assisted firing position

2-42. Troops use special firing procedures when employing crew-served weapons in the snow. If they set the weapon down in the snow with just the tripod or bipod, it will sink. Depending on the depth of the snow, the weapon can sink to a point where the snow covers it and a malfunction occurs. Soldiers and Marines can use various methods to provide a stable platform for the weapon system. Common techniques include using the ahkio (or any sled) as a platform or an extra snowshoe (classic type) as use as a base (see figure 2-11). Other easy techniques include doubling the box sleeve from the meals-ready-to-eat. A platform at least 18 by 14 inches (46 by 36 centimeters) provides a stable platform.

2-43. The gunner and assistant gunner ensure the belt-fed ammunition clears the snow. If the rounds carry snow into the weapon system, the bolt will malfunction. If possible, personnel carry ammunition in their metal cases to their firing positions. However, this is not likely when conducting patrols due to the bulky nature of ammunition cases and their weight. Carrying belt fed ammunition in soft pouches works effectively. Personnel have easy access to soft pouches.

2-44. Most Soldiers and Marines operating in cold region environments use snowshoes. To maintain noise discipline, leaders, Soldiers, and Marines carefully consider which type of snowshoe to use when conducting patrols. The classic style snowshoe shown in figure 2-12 (commonly known as the tennis-racket or magnesium) does not generate much noise when moving through snow. However, this system makes travels slower than the contemporary design. It also does not provide as much traction as the modular steel traction snowshoe (MSTS) shown in figure 2-13. As a general rule, Soldiers are phasing out this type of snowshoe in favor of the MSTS-type snowshoe as shown in figure 2-13. The Marine Corps does not use the classic snowshoe (magnesium) shown in figure 2-12. Instead, they use the MSTS shown in figure 2-13 on page 2-12.

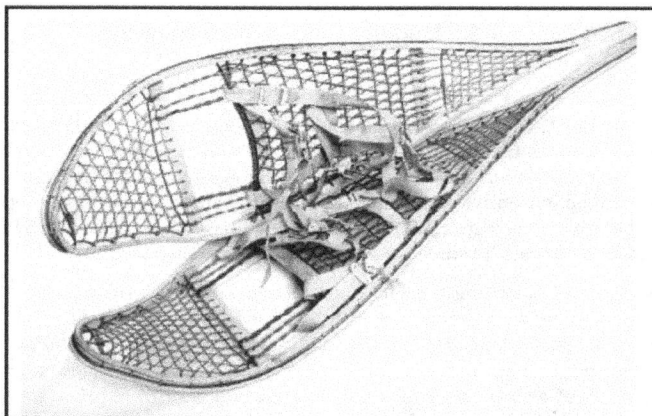

Figure 2-12. Classic snow shoe

2-45. Units located in Alaska use the MSTS streamlined type snowshoe. The MSTS has a narrower construction. This smaller width provides an easier range of motion and greater traction. Personnel can easily remove or put on the snowshoes due to the universal design of the straps that secure the boot to the snowshoe. Two disadvantages to this system involve noise and fasteners. These snowshoes generate more noise when moving over snow. Personnel also need to carry additional straps since the rubber straps become brittle and break off at temperatures at or below -20 °F (-29 °C).

Figure 2-13. Modular steel traction snowshoe

Deception

2-46. Many opportunities exist for unit or individual deception in cold regions during winter. However, deception measures are not sufficiently effective to lessen the requirement for good concealment. Unless units and individuals use camouflage effectively, they greatly reduce the value of any deception plan. Leaders must base deception on well-coordinated plans that are logical and not too obvious. Units use dummy positions that follow the tactical plan. They use positions far enough removed from actual positions so that fire directed at the dummy position does not endanger the real position.

2-47. Snowshoes, skis, and over-snow vehicles can create a network of trails or tracks to mislead the enemy as to direction, strength, location, and intentions of friendly forces. Troops can make improvised explosive devices from snow, branches, canvas, and any other available material. Units can construct dummy weapons, positions, tents, and vehicles of all kinds. Dummies must appear camouflaged and only "discovered" as a result of a camouflage violation. Units can use small gasoline or oil flames to simulate stoves or idling engines. A dummy patrol base area must appear occupied; units can use a fire or smoke to produce this effect. Units also gain deception or concealment by deliberately creating vapor fogs or clouds.

DEFENSIVE OPERATIONS

2-48. *Defensive operations* are combat operations conducted to defeat an enemy, attack, gain time, economize forces, and develop conditions favorable for offensive or stability operations (FM 3-0). Marines conduct defensive operations to defeat an enemy attack, gain time or economize forces, and develop conditions favorable to offensive and stability operations. Three types of defensive maneuver consist of position, mobile, and retrograde. Due to the restrictive nature of the cold region environment and extended lines of communication, commanders may be forced to operate in the defense to restore combat power or allow logistic elements time to resupply combat units.

TYPES OF DEFENSIVE OPERATIONS

2-49. The defense in the cold region environment offers many opportunities and challenges. Often a delicate balance exists between maintaining mobile and static defenses. This balance depends on the season and time of year. No matter what type of defense units employ, a battle centers on denying the enemy the ability to maneuver along avenues of approach. Units take care not to facilitate enemy movement by staying on established trail networks. If personnel create additional trail networks, it makes it easier for the enemy to determine strength, composition, and disposition.

Area Defense (Army)/Position Defense (USMC)

2-50. During the spring break up, summer, and early fall, conditions favor the area defense because trafficability is poor for the attacker. Letting the enemy attack a robust network of well-prepared positions and then counterattacking may prove the best course of action. Such a course of action exposes enemy forces to the elements, especially if the enemy lacks warming equipment and other logistic support.

2-51. Commanders carefully consider the terrain, weather, and temperature range before choosing a defense scheme that emphasizes static elements. Area defenses cause problems since they require additional construction time to build fighting positions and obstacles. The need to keep Soldiers and Marines heated in extremely cold temperatures also complicates matters.

Mobile Defense

2-52. Leaders often find that conditions favor a mobile defense during the winter months. Since the ground freezes during this time of year, offensive forces move and maneuver more easily on the battlefield. A mobile defense is hard to maintain in spring, summer, and fall due to the marshy terrain. The size and capabilities of the reserve become the paramount concern for this type of operation.

Employment of the Reserve

2-53. The employment of the reserve takes on special importance in the cold region environment. Leaders ensure reserve forces receive proper training in cold region environment movement techniques using skis or snowshoes to facilitate rapid closure with enemy forces. If reserve forces lack specialized movement equipment, units must prepare routes to facilitate mobility along likely enemy avenues of approach. Commanders place the major portion of the reserve in covered and concealed positions, protected from enemy artillery fire, while placing the remainder closer to the front lines. Units prepare trails and roads to the probable points of action for the reserve troops. Elements of the reserve then keep these trails and roads open during snowstorms. So far as is possible, troops camouflage the roads and trails.

2-54. Once units identify avenues of approach, they can then maneuver to provide favorable force ratios. If friendly forces defend a broad front, they need to define the enemy avenues of approach and enemy strengths on each avenue early. Mutual support on a wide front may become problematic due to large distances inherent in cold region environments. If gaps exist, reconnaissance assets (or sensors if there is a lack of personnel) keep the area under surveillance. Commanders develop effective fire plans to cover these gaps.

Countermobility Operations

2-55. In cold region environments, avenues of approach are the key to victory. Retaining control over limited road and trail networks proves instrumental in allowing forces to advance in a theater of war. The obstacles in summer—lakes, rivers, swamps, or bogs—often become avenues of approach for enemy forces and complicate the defense scheme of friendly commanders. These areas lengthen the front line of a given area of operation, requiring more troops and weapons to defend it than in summer. Commanders take action to deny these natural routes to the enemy under winter conditions. Soldiers and Marines use this information with discussions from FM 3-34, FM 5-34, FM 5-102, FM 90-7, and MCWP 3-17.

Denying Access To Waterways

2-56. Commanders eliminate many planning variables in their defensive scheme by nullifying waterways as an avenue of approach. To create water obstacles during winter conditions, units use explosives to blow gaps in lake and river ice making it impassable to enemy personnel and armor. To install an explosive in ice, personnel sink holes 10 feet (3 meters) apart in staggered rows with axes, chisels, ice augers, steam point drilling equipment. Figure 2-14 illustrates how to execute this technique.

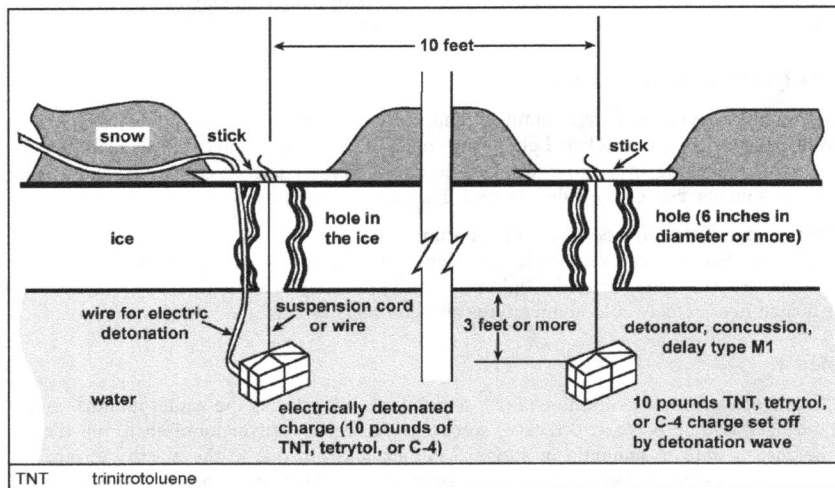

Figure 2-14. Method of placing charges in ice

2-57. Soldiers and Marines suspend the charges in the water below the ice with cords tied to sticks bridging the tops of the holes. The charges should be of an explosive not affected by water. Soldiers and Marines protect plastic explosives from erosion by water currents. Early in the winter, personnel lay demolitions deep enough so that they will not be encased in the ice as it grows thicker.

2-58. The normal thickness of fresh water ice is approximately 4 feet (120 centimeters) or less. In extremely cold areas, 5 feet (150 centimeters) of ice is not uncommon. When units establish the minefield, they cannot always determine how thick the ice will form when detonating the ice demolition. Generally, if they expect the ice to be 4 feet (120 centimeters) thick, they build charges to approximately 10 pounds. In the event units expect the depth of the ice to exceed 4 feet (120 centimeters), they emplace an additional 2.5 pounds per additional 1 foot (30 centimeters) of thickness. Personnel attach electrical firing devices to three charges in each underwater demolition, one in each end charge and one in the middle charge. They prime the rest of the charges with concussion detonators or electrically prime them. The large number of charges limits the use of electrical means of firing. An ice demolition may consist of several blocks of charges echeloned in width and depth and has at least two rows of mines, each row alternating with the one before it. Blowing a demolition such as this creates an obstacle for enemy armor and vehicles for approximately 24 hours at -24 °F (-31 °C).

2-59. Soldiers and Marines exercise great care when handling electrical firing devices under winter conditions. Because of improper grounding of an individual caused by the snow and ice on the ground, the static electricity that builds up might detonate the device. Individuals must ensure that they are properly grounded before handling any type of electrical firing devices. They also ensure that no radio transmitters are operating in the immediate area. The type of radio signals emitted by this type of equipment can detonate electrical firing devices.

2-60. Placing charges in ice has the following advantages:

- Units can cut off long areas of the front line at a critical moment from enemy infantry and armor.
- Units require fewer resources to defend a given area.

- Friendly troops may advance or withdraw at any place over the charges without being restricted to the cleared lanes.
- Charges laid under thick ice are difficult, and often impossible, to detect by use of mine detectors.
- When the holes over the charges have refrozen, the field is difficult for the enemy to breach.
- Charges are not affected by weather or snow conditions.

2-61. Placing charges in ice has the following disadvantages:

- Emplacing explosives requires considerable time even when troops have ice cutting equipment.
- Charges can be set off when hit by artillery fire.
- Gaps blown in the ice tend to freeze over rapidly in low temperatures.
- Continued exposure of the demolition firing system to weather reduces the reliability of the system.

2-62. Units use ice demolitions for protection from frontal or flanking attacks. Normally, units lay one or more sets of charges close to the friendly shore and others farther out in the direction of the enemy. If desired, units allow the enemy to advance past the first set of charges and then detonate both at the same time. The enemy thus will be marooned on an ice floe, unable to continue to advance or retreat, and can be destroyed. Units can use the same trapping method against enemy armor, or detonate the charges directly under advancing tanks. Commanders keep ice demolitions under observation and secured by friendly fire.

2-63. Ice breaching denies the enemy use of frozen waterways as an avenue of approach. To properly create a water obstacle in this way, units must first construct a detailed engineer reconnaissance.

CONSTRUCTING OBSTACLES

2-64. Troops can use obstacles to disrupt, fix, turn, or block the movement of an opposing force, and to impose additional losses in personnel, time, and equipment. Obstacles are classified as natural or man-made. In cold region environments, units can use either obstacle type or a combination of the two to hinder and restrict enemy maneuver.

Natural Obstacles

2-65. One of the most important natural obstacles that Soldiers and Marines can use in cold region environments is slope. A steep slope is an obstacle to troops and vehicles even under normal conditions. When covered by deep snow or ice, it becomes much harder to surmount. The bogging-down action and the loss of traction caused by deep snow frequently creates obstacles out of slopes that personnel might easily overcome otherwise.

2-66. An avalanche makes an excellent obstacle for blocking passes and roads. However, this type of obstacle is only available in hilly or mountainous terrain with few natural avenues of approach. An avalanche can have a far-reaching influence over combat operations. However, avalanches that occur naturally may help the enemy unless their timing and location are just right. Units can predict where an avalanche can and probably will occur. By using artillery fire, bombs, or explosives, units might induce the avalanche to slide at the desired time. This type avalanche is an artificial obstacle in the technical sense. Generally, it will be of more value than the natural type.

2-67. Windfalls are another natural obstacle that precludes movement and maneuver. These occur when strong winds knock over trees in a wooded area. These obstacles reduce the effectiveness of personnel who wear skis and even snowshoes. Covering windfall with snow enhances the effectiveness of this technique.

Man-Made Obstacles

2-68. Man-made obstacles include abatises, wires, and ice. An abatis is similar to a windfall. Units fell trees at an angle of about 45 degrees to the enemy's direction of approach leaving the stump attached to hamper removal. Along trails, roads, and slopes, abatises can cause much trouble for skiers and vehicles. Units can also use wire obstacles (concertina and single strand) to great effect. Another useful obstacle units can make involves pouring water on road grades. The ice that forms will seriously hamper vehicular traffic. FM 3-34, FM 5-34, FM 5-102, and FM 90-7 discuss techniques of man-made obstacles.

RETROGRADE OPERATIONS

2-69. Units execute retrograde operations in the same manner as they do in more temperate climates. In cold region environments, units frequently have suitable conditions for leaving strong combat patrols up to a strength of one or two platoons to harass or ambush the advancing enemy. Units can launch surprise attacks against columns of vehicles and troops at natural defiles.

2-70. When troops must delay or withdraw, the cold region environment battlefield favors the defender. Defending forces often know the terrain. Further, they are better prepared to cope with mobility and trafficability problems than the attacking force. Mobility problems often make a passage of lines more difficult to coordinate and control. Commanders must pay extra attention to identification of vehicles, routes of passage, signals, and coordination of movements.

2-71. While conducting retrograde operations is never the preferred option, it sometimes becomes necessary in the cold region environment. The Marine Corps' performance at the Chosin Reservoir withdrawal best illustrates this. In the winter of 1950, 20,000 United Nations (UN) troops found themselves cut off and surrounded by over 200,000 Chinese forces. The cold affected both sides in the fight. Temperatures reached -48 °F. However, UN forces successfully withdrew to the port of Hungnam. UN forces suffered 2,500 killed, 5,000 wounded, and 7,500 frostbite victims, but in the end the cold took a much heavier toll on the Chinese. The Chinese suffered ten times the number of dead as UN forces with 12,500 wounded and 30,000 frostbite victims.

STABILITY OPERATIONS

2-72. *Stability operations* encompass various military missions, tasks, and activities conducted outside the United States in coordination with other instruments of power to maintain or reestablish a safe and secure environment, provide essential government services, emergency infrastructure reconstruction, and humanitarian relief (joint publication [JP] 3-0). FM 3-0 and FM 3-07 outline activities for stability operations. Units execute the methods outlined in these manuals in the same manner anywhere, regardless of the environmental conditions. However, when conducting operations in the cold region environment, certain aspects of restoring and providing essential services differ from those found in warmer regions.

2-73. Many of the same factors that limit offensive and defensive operations impact stability operations. Extended lines of communication, lack of rail networks and airports, difficult terrain and weather, and limited road networks limit the amount of logistic support the Army can deliver in support of civilian populations. In addition to these limitations, units need many transportation assets to maintain the force, especially if forces are engaged in on-going operations.

2-74. Soldiers and Marines concentrate on six key tasks to restore essential services to the population in the cold region environment. These factors are—
- Providing emergency medical care and rescue.
- Preventing epidemic disease.
- Providing food and water.
- Providing emergency shelter.
- Providing basic sanitation (sewage and garbage disposal).
- Providing a source of heat.

2-75. All environments require the first five tasks and are mentioned in FM 3-0. In addition to this, units provide a way to keep individuals warm. Commanders meet this task by providing clothing appropriate for the climate, a heat source such as an approved stove, or ideally, both of these items. Providing shelter and a form of warmth are key in the cold region environment since 80 percent of dislocated civilians are women and children.

2-76. Potentially this problem is limited since many cold regions have relatively small populations. Smaller populations in turn require far fewer resources than large populations demand. However, exceptions to this rule exist—such as Korea and Europe—which contain large populations.

2-77. Commanders address engineer concerns before they commence and maintain stability operations. For example, in 1995, before beginning Operation Joint Endeavor, 20,000 Soldiers had to cross the Sava River into

Bosnia-Herzegovina after the bridges were destroyed. This problem was compounded since the Army undertook this operation during the worst Balkan winter in 70 years and the river was flooding. An improvised float bridge served as a critical lifeline for the operation for six months until more semipermanent structures could be repaired.

CIVIL SUPPORT OPERATIONS

2-78. *Civil support* is Department of Defense support to U.S. civil authorities for domestic emergencies, and for designated law enforcement and other activities (JP 3-28). When Army units engage in civil support operations in a cold region, specially trained units with cold region expertise will execute them, usually National Guard. Examples of this include cold weather air rescue operations. In extreme circumstances, Regular Army or U.S. Army Reserve forces augment state and local resources. In certain cold regions, federal agencies and state and local authorities have developed mutually beneficial relationships. These relationships provide the Army with valuable training opportunities. In addition, these relationships foster positive civil-military relationships and can help reduce the cost to state and local government agencies. However, these relationships can be suspended due to operational commitments such as deployments to a contingency operation. Marines can utilize the Marine Corps assets in many of the same civil support roles if tasked by Headquarters, Marine Corps. An incident command staff and commander will utilize both Army and Marine Corps units. Soldiers reference FM 3-28 for more information.

This page intentionally left blank.

Chapter 3

Considerations for Operations in Cold Regions

Individual and small-unit training and indoctrination provide the fundamental framework for successful operations in the cold region environment. This chapter covers the basic principles for personnel, weapons, and tactics for cold region operations.

PERSONNEL CONSIDERATIONS

3-1. Cold conditions injure and kill Soldiers and Marines in war. In World War II, U.S. forces suffered nearly 85,000 cold weather casualties. During the Korean War, almost 10,000 U.S. forces suffered cold injuries. Studies show that the human body adapts poorly to the cold region environment. Experts have found no way to enhance physiological cold tolerance through exposure to cold regions. To prevent cold injuries, leaders at all levels must understand the unique individual requirements and peculiar environmental hazards of operating in the cold region environment. Soldiers and Marines must put this knowledge to use in the field to develop the skill set that enables them to function in the cold and focus on the mission.

3-2. Individual care can easily become the most important aspect of combat power in the cold region environment. The cold region environment can easily disrupt the delicate heat balance that the human body must maintain. Even small deviations from the average 98.6 °F (37 °C) body core temperature will impair physical and mental performance. For further discussion on cold weather injuries, Soldiers refer to technical bulletin (TB) medical (MED) 508. Marines refer to MCRP 3-35.1A.

ENVIRONMENTAL RISK FACTORS

3-3. Weather is the primary environmental hazard to individual Soldiers and Marines. Leaders look at current and forecast weather conditions regularly as a part of the planning process. Wind has a pronounced effect on the temperature experienced by Soldiers and Marines—this is known as the wind chill effect.

3-4. Leaders use a wind chill chart (see table 3-1 on page 3-2) to determine a wind chill temperature. The wind chill temperature is the equivalent still air temperature (without wind) at which the heat loss through bare skin would be the same as under the windy conditions. This tool also allows commanders to assess conditions (both current and forecast) to determine the likelihood of frostbite occurring under those conditions.

Table 3-1. Wind chill chart

	Temperature (°F)																		
	Calm	40	35	30	25	20	15	10	5	0	-5	-10	-15	-20	-25	-30	-35	-40	-45
Wind Speed (mph)	5	36	31	25	19	13	7	1	-5	-11	-16	-22	-28	-34	-40	-46	-52	-57	-63
	10	34	27	21	15	9	3	-4	-10	-16	-22	-28	-35	-41	-47	-53	-59	-66	-72
	15	32	25	19	13	6	0	-7	-13	-19	-26	-32	-39	-45	-51	-58	-64	-71	-77
	20	30	24	17	11	4	-2	-9	-15	-22	-29	-35	-42	-48	-55	-61	-68	-74	-81
	25	29	23	16	9	3	-4	-11	-17	-24	-31	-37	-44	-51	-58	-64	-71	-78	-84
	30	28	22	15	8	1	-5	-12	-19	-26	-33	-39	-46	-53	-60	-67	-73	-80	-87
	35	28	21	14	7	0	-7	-14	-21	-27	-34	-41	-48	-55	-62	-69	-76	-82	-89
	40	27	20	13	6	-1	-8	-15	-22	-29	-36	-43	-50	-57	-64	-71	-78	-84	-91
	45	26	19	12	5	-2	-9	-16	-23	-30	-37	-44	-51	-58	-65	-72	-79	-86	-93
	50	26	19	12	4	-3	-10	-17	-24	-31	-38	-45	-52	-60	-67	-74	-81	-88	-95
	55	25	18	11	4	-3	-11	-18	-25	-32	-39	-46	-54	-61	-68	-75	-82	-89	-97
	60	25	17	10	3	-4	-11	-19	-26	-33	-40	-48	-55	-62	-69	-76	-84	-91	-98

Frostbite Times: Light Grey = 30 Minutes Medium Grey = 10 Minutes Dark Grey = 5 Minutes
Wind Chill (°F) = 35.74 + 0.6215T - 35.75 ($V^{0.16}$) + 0.4275T ($V^{0.16}$)
Where, T = Air Temperature (°F) V = Wind Speed (MPH)

3-5. Wet skin will significantly decrease the time for frostbite to occur. Wind even further exacerbates this problem. Wet skin and wind create a wet skin wind chill. Soldiers and Marines use table 3-2 to determine wet skin wind chill.

3-6. Rotor wash can create dangerously low wind chill temperatures. Troops exposed to the elements when moving in uncovered or drafty vehicles can also experience dangerous wind chill conditions.

3-7. Skin cannot freeze (so frostbite cannot occur) at temperatures above 32 °F (0 °C), even when the equivalent wind chill temperature is below 32 °F (0 °C).

Table 3-2. Wet wind chill chart

Wind Speed (MPH)	Air Temperature (°F)											
	10	5	0	-5	-10	-15	-20	-25	-30	-35	-40	-45
5	>120	>120	>120	>120	31	22	17	14	12	11	9	8
10	>120	>120	>120	28	19	15	12	10	9	7	7	6
15	>120	>120	33	20	15	12	9	8	7	6	5	4
20	>120	>120	23	16	12	9	8	8	6	5	4	4
25	>120	42	19	13	10	8	7	6	5	4	4	3
30	>120	28	16	12	9	7	6	5	4	4	3	3
35	>120	23	14	10	8	6	5	4	4	3	3	2
40	>120	20	13	9	7	6	5	4	3	3	2	2
45	>120	18	12	8	7	5	4	4	3	3	2	2
50	>120	16	11	8	6	5	4	3	3	2	2	2

Note: Wet skin significantly decreases the time for frostbite to occur.
FROSTBITE RISK
LOW – freezing is possible, but unlikely (white)
HIGH – freezing could occur in 10-30 minutes (light grey)
SEVERE – freezing could occur in 5-10 minutes (dark grey)
EXTREME – freezing could occur in <5 minutes (medium grey)

MISSION RISK FACTORS

3-8. Planners and leaders consider many factors when planning for operations in cold regions including:

- Mission type, activity level and duration of exposure to the environment.
- Availability of heated shelters.
- Availability of food and water.
- Availability of the proper clothing and equipment.

INDIVIDUAL RISK FACTORS

3-9. Risk factors for individuals consist of differences between the person's heat gain and heat loss as well as how individual bodies respond to heat loss.

Heat Gain Versus Heat Loss

3-10. The human body maintains a relatively constant core temperature by balancing heat gain from the environment and metabolism with heat loss. When the two are equal, very little heat loss occurs and the body can maintain a body core temperature that averages 98.6 °F (37 °C).

Heat Gain

3-11. Basal metabolism produces heat as the body consumes energy to maintain basic life functions. At rest this is known as the basal metabolic rate. Normal daily activities also generate heat. Vigorous exercise generates up to 18 times the normal basal metabolic rate; this is known as exercise metabolism. External heat sources such as the sun, fires, and stoves can also cause the human body to experience heat gain, though not to a great extent.

Heat Loss

3-12. Five components relate to heat loss between the body and the environment: radiation, conduction, convection, respiration, and evaporation. Table 3-3 provides approximate values of how much heat loss occurs through these components.

Table 3-3. Heat loss components

Heat Loss Methods	Percentage of Total Loss
Radiation	60 percent
Convection	Variable
Conduction	Variable
Respiration	6–10 percent
Evaporation	12–15 percent

3-13. **Radiation** is the normal loss of body heat to the surrounding air. This is direct energy emission usually in the form of infrared radiation. Clothing manufacturers have tried to create clothing that recaptures this lost heat without much success (such as the space blanket). This form of heat loss is hard to prevent. Even with the best clothing for cold regions, radiated heat transfers to the clothing and then out to the surrounding atmosphere. This form of heat loss generally does not become an issue until temperatures reach -20° F (-29 °C).

3-14. **Conduction** and **convection** both involve the transfer of heat energy between two objects of different temperatures that contact one another. These forms of heat loss prove the most dangerous to Soldiers and Marines. Fortunately, cold weather clothing and equipment reduce the effects of heat loss from conduction and convection. Conduction occurs as heat is transferred from a warm object to a cold object. When personnel lie down on cold, bare ground, they lose heat to the ground. Convective heat loss occurs as a surrounding colder medium (air or water) is heated by the skin. This type of heat loss is generally negligible in temperate climates. *In cold climates, convective heat loss is the major contributor to heat loss.* Wind increases the effects of convective cooling by maintaining the temperature difference between the body and the air. The stronger the winds, the faster heat is stripped away from the body; the amount of heat extracted by moving air increases as the square of the velocity. This effect is the wind chill discussed in paragraph 3-3.

3-15. **Respiration** is the loss of body heat (and water loss) as an individual breathes. Evaporative heat loss occurs as a Soldier or Marine sweats and the sweat converts from a liquid to a gas.

3-16. **Evaporation** of sweat is a form of heat loss. In a cold region environment, excessive sweating can result from increased physical activity and inadequate adjustments to clothing for cold regions.

Body Response to Heat Loss

3-17. If the body is exposed to the cold, and heat loss occurs, the balance is disrupted. In response to heat loss, vasoconstriction (constriction of blood vessels) in the extremities (shell) occurs. This restricts blood flow to the shell and increases the blood volume in the torso (core). This shell-core effect protects the vital internal organs from heat loss. One estimation of the protection that this provides to the core equals that of putting on a light business suit. Reduced blood flow to the extremities can hasten the onset of frostbite and decreases manual dexterity.

3-18. Due to the shell-core effect, the kidneys sense an increase in blood volume and convert some of the fluid volume to urine. The increase in blood volume in the core may also disrupt the thirst mechanism. Increased urine output in the cold region environment results; this is known as cold induced diuresis. Coupled with the fact that individuals have a tendency to drink less in a cold region environment, the overall effect can be dehydration.

3-19. Cold induced vasodilation (CIVD), sometimes referred to as hunters response, will periodically increase the flow of blood to extremities thereby increasing the skin temperature of fingers, toes, ears, nose, and other body parts. Individuals routinely exposed to cold and can maintain proper core temperatures with adequate clothing and activity levels typically have a more pronounced CIVD response. Most people experience CIVD. It is thought to positively counteract the negative effect of lower extremity skin temperatures associated with the shell-core effect.

3-20. The last way the body responds to heat loss is shivering thermo genesis. If the shell-core effect does not counteract heat loss and individuals do not take voluntary steps to reduce heat loss, the body begins to shiver. Heat production (thermo genesis) from shivering can be up to six times the resting metabolic rate. Uncontrolled shivering can significantly impact coordination.

INDIVIDUAL FACTORS

3-21. Individual differences can make a Soldier or Marine more or less susceptible to cold injuries. For example, the body composition of some individuals seems able to maintain body core temperatures better than others. Short and stocky individuals have a smaller skin surface area and are less prone to heat loss than taller, leaner individuals. Body fat also provides better insulation than other body tissues. Those with higher body fat composition typically lose less heat to the environment. See TB MED 508 (Marines refer to MCRP 3-35.1A) for further discussion regarding these categories. Leaders need to keep in mind the following indicators:

- Fitness level.
- Age.
- Gender and race.
- Prior cold injuries.
- Drugs and alcohol.
- Food and water.
- Personal hygiene.

Fitness Level

3-22. The level of fitness level does not directly affect the individual's ability to handle the cold. However, Soldiers and Marines with a high fitness level can to sustain work for longer periods before fatigue sets in. These personnel also recover faster and are often less susceptible to injury or illness.

Age

3-23. Age has been shown to play a role in the susceptibility of personnel to cold injuries. Soldiers and Marines older than 45 years of age may suffer the effects of cold more readily than younger Soldiers and Marines. Recent data has shown that cold injury rates are higher in young males from warm climates with less than eighteen months of service.

Gender and Race

3-24. Women sustain twice the number of peripheral cold injuries than men. African-American male and females sustain two to four times the number of cold injuries than their Caucasian counterparts. These gender and race differences stem from variability in body composition.

Prior Cold Injuries

3-25. Soldiers and Marines who have sustained cold injuries in the past have an increased risk for similar injuries in the future. Unit standard operating procedures need to dictate a marking system to ensure that these individuals can be easily identified for monitoring. See table 4-1 in TB MED 508 (Marines refer to MCRP 3-35.1A) for further discussion.

Drugs, Tobacco, and Alcohol

3-26. Drugs, tobacco, and alcohol use can be a contributing factor to cold injuries. Some prescription drugs may contain substances that will increase the likelihood of cold injuries. Tobacco acts as a vasoconstrictor and can potentially increase the likelihood of cold injuries to extremities. Alcohol can create an artificial feeling of warmth, mask the symptoms of cold injuries, and suppress normal body reactions to the cold.

Food and Water

3-27. Fluid requirements during cold-weather training vary according to physical activity levels. Most people need to consume about 3 to 6 quarts (2.8 and 5.6 liters) per day. This includes the water in food. The best time for personnel to rehydrate is at mealtime. Soldiers and Marines usually drink most of their water with meals, and eating food improves water consumption. Leaders must provide Soldiers and Marines with adequate time for meals and fluids. In addition, meals provide the salt intake necessary to retain body water.

3-28. Soldiers and Marines store canteens upside down to prevent freezing at the opening. Commercial off-the-shelf, wide-mouth bottles with insulated carriers also work well. If used, personnel store these items upside down like canteens. Personal hydration systems work poorly at temperatures below -5 °F (-20 °C). Below this temperature, these systems tend to accumulate ice and burst or leak at the bladders, soaking clothing. If units use these systems, individuals do the following to ensure these systems function properly:

- Keep the bladder between layers one and two or between the insulating layer and the outer shell layer of clothing. This keeps both the water and plastic from freezing, especially during movement when body heat will keep the water warm. Never store this system in a rucksack, assault pack, or on the outside of the shell layer exposed to the elements.
- Blow back into the drinking straw to clear all water from the line when done drinking, then use the "on/off" valve to close off any additional air. Although air does not freeze, water does. Freezing water breaks drinking tubes.
- Route the drinking tube along the inside sleeve of the outer shell layer to keep from being exposed to the wind or snow.

3-29. Soldiers and Marines require 4,500 kilocalories per day in a cold region environment. This is a 10 to 40 percent caloric increase over normal requirements. Four meals-ready-to-eat (MREs) provide approximately 4,500 kilocalories (1,250 kilocalories per MRE). MRE components will freeze and can be difficult to re-heat in the field. Troops must use MREs or discard them after one freeze-thaw cycle. MREs only average about 7 ounces (.2 liters) of fluid per meal (less than ¼ quart), so individuals get less than 1 quart (1 liter) total fluid from four MREs.

3-30. The meal, cold weather (MCW) is designed for cold region operations. It will not freeze and provides extra drink mixes for countering dehydration during cold region activities. Three MCWs per day provides approximately 4,500 kilocalories (1,450 kilocalories each). One MCW requires just over 1 quart (1 liter) of water to re-hydrate all its parts.

3-31. For units that operate away from a support base, Soldiers and Marines can use small, commercially available, multi-fuel stoves to melt snow for drinking water and to rehydrate rations. Commanders highly encourage use of a stove since it will keep individuals from carrying heavy loads of water. A minimum of two of these stoves per squad suffices. Soldiers and Marines must bring the water to a rolling boil to destroy waterborne pathogens. To conserve fuel, individuals can melt and then treat snow or ice with iodine or other water purification means. Refer to FM 4-25.12 and FM 21-10 for additional guidance on water purification methods.

Personal Hygiene

3-32. Often personnel neglect personal hygiene and field sanitation in cold regions. Food and water needs often take precedence over personal hygiene. Because of the extremes in temperatures and lack of bathing and sanitary facilities, keeping the body clean in a cold region environment is not an easy proposition. Still, Soldiers and Marines need to attend to hygiene in the cold region environment. Soldiers can reference FM 4-25.12 and FM 21-10 for a more robust sanitation technique listing. Marines refer to MCRP 4-11.1D.

3-33. Soldiers and Marines should shave daily and not allow hair to grow too long. A beard and longer hair adds little insulation and soils clothing with natural hair oils. In winter, a beard or a mustache becomes a nuisance since it serves as a base for the build-up of ice from moisture in the breath and hides the presence of frostbite. Shave daily when possible. Because shaving with a blade and soap removes protective face oils, shave several hours before exposure to the elements to reduce the danger of frostbite, usually at the beginning of the rest cycle. Shaving with an electric razor will not remove the protective oils.

3-34. Soldiers and Marines should wash their entire body weekly (at a minimum). If bathing facilities are not available, individuals can wash with two canteen cups of water, using half for soap and washing and half for rinsing. They must clean feet, crotch, and armpits daily. They should also clean teeth daily. It is important that Soldiers and Marines do not use alcohol-based wipes (commonly known as baby wipes) in the field. These wipes contain alcohol that will be the same temperature as the ambient air. If individuals use these products in an environment where the temperature is below freezing, then they risk contact frostbite, especially if the temperature is below 0 °F (-18 °C).

3-35. Soldiers and Marines should change socks once per day at a minimum. If this is not possible, they should remove boots and socks and then dry and massage feet once per day.

3-36. Units pack out, burn, or bury accumulated garbage. For the small unit, the preferred method is to keep trash generated from rations and other sources with the individual. As the unit is re-supplied periodically, the unit collects and disposes this garbage in a land-fill or by incineration. For temporary living areas of more than one week, personnel can burn garbage in open incinerators. Soldiers see FM 4-25.12 for techniques. Marines refer to MCRP 4-11.1D. Burial is the least preferred method because it is nearly impossible to dig pits in frozen ground and the trash may adversely affect the environment.

3-37. For units on the move, Soldiers and Marines can use individual waste collection bags. Units position field latrines downwind from patrol base areas and at least 100 meters from any food service areas or water and snow collection points. For patrol bases of less than one week, personnel should construct the cross-tree type latrine. They collect solid waste using a ration box lined with a double trash bag or a commercially available pail and bag. A windbreak of boughs, tarps, ponchos, or snow-wall protects the latrine from wind and provides some privacy. The latrine area should be clearly marked. Prior to striking camp, units collect or burn the human waste for disposal in a land-fill. A urinal, designated for each shelter, should be located within 13 to 16 feet (4 to 5 meters) of the shelter. For living areas that units intend to occupy for longer than one week, the burn out method for solid waste is appropriate in the cold region environment. If units will haul human waste back, they must mark it "Human Waste" and transport it apart from class I supplies.

COLD INJURIES

3-38. Cold injuries affect Soldiers and Marines in the cold region environment. Leaders, Soldiers, and Marines should be aware of these injuries to prevent them and treat them if necessary.

Hypothermia

3-39. Hypothermia occurs when core body temperature falls below 95 °F (35 °C). Hypothermia is characterized as mild, moderate, or severe based on core body temperature. Mild hypothermia occurs when the core body temperature is between 90 °F and 95 °F (32 °C and 35 °C). Moderate hypothermia occurs at core body temperatures between 80 °F to 89 °F (27 °C to 32 °C). Severe hypothermia exists when the core body temperature falls below 80 °F (27 °C). Rectal temperature measurement provides the only accurate core body temperature. Since Soldiers and Marines will not likely use this method in the field, they should make their diagnoses using obvious signs and symptoms. All levels of hypothermia are potentially life threatening medical emergencies and require immediate care in a medical facility.

3-40. Often exposure to cold, wet, or cold and wet conditions causes hypothermia. U.S. forces must know symptoms of with immersion syndrome, warning signs of hypothermia, symptoms and treatment of hypothermia, and prevention.

Immersion Syndrome

3-41. Immersion syndrome is a nonfreezing cold injury developed by tissues exposed to cold-wet conditions—usually between 32 °F and 60 °F (0 °C an 16 °C)—for prolonged periods (about 4 to 5 days minimum). It can occur in any tissue but occurs most often in the feet. In extreme cold region environments, individuals who wear vapor barrier boots for long periods with wet socks often develop immersion syndrome. Feet initially appear swollen and red with a feeling of numbness. The tissue may become pale in more serious injuries. Often, aches, increased pain sensitivity, and infections accompanied immersion syndrome.

3-42. Soldiers and Marines treat victims of immersion syndrome by—
- Preventing further exposure.
- Removing wet or constrictive clothing.
- Washing and drying extremities gently.
- Elevating and covering limbs with layers of loose, warm, dry clothing.
- Evacuating to a medical facility.
- Touching affected areas carefully. They do not pop blisters, apply lotions, massage, expose to extreme heat, or have the individual walk.

3-43. To prevent immersion syndrome, Soldiers and Marines—
- Keep feet warm and dry. They change wet socks as soon as possible.
- As mission permits, remove boots and allow feet to dry out for 2 to 3 hours, at a minimum, per day.
- Wipe the inside of vapor barrier boots dry at least once per day or more often as feet sweat.

3-44. Soldiers and Marines can also keep boots dry by placing the boots in their sleeping bags at night when sleeping. The individual's body heat will dry the boots and keep them pliable for use the next day. If available, Soldiers and Marines may also place an absorbent synthetic chamois towel or paper towels in boots overnight to draw out moisture. Troops can use these techniques with either leather boots or the vapor barrier boot.

3-45. Table 3-4 presents the allowable exposure time during immersion at various water temperatures and immersion depths. These exposure times reflect the time it takes the body core temperature to fall to

95.9 °F (35.5 °C). The size of average personnel determines immersion time limits. Leaders recognize that some Soldiers and Marines will cool faster than the time limits predicted by the table. Personnel who have low body fat and a high surface-area-to-mass ratio are susceptible to cooling more quickly. Personnel who have not eaten in over 24 hours are more susceptible, as are those who are fatigued because of physical exhaustion or sustained operations. Time limits when immersed to the neck are very short to avoid the possibility of drowning.

Table 3-4. Immersion chart

Water Temperature (in degrees F)	Ankle-Deep	Knee-Deep	Waist-Deep	Neck
50–54	7 hours If raining, 3.5 hours	5 hours If raining, 2.5 hours	1.5 hours If raining, 1 hr	5 minutes
55–59	8 hours If raining, 4 hours	7 hours If raining, 3.5 hours	2 hours If raining, 1.5 hours	5 minutes
60–64	9 hours If raining, 4.5 hours	8 hours If raining, 4 hours	3.5 hours If raining, 2.5 hours	10 minutes
65–69	12 hours If raining, 6 hours	12 hours If raining, 6 hours	6 hours If raining, 5 hours	10 minutes
>70	No limit	No limit	No limit	30 minutes

Warning Signs

3-46. Warning signs appear as hypothermia starts to set in. As the core body temperature begins to fall, shivering will be the most noticeable symptom. Shivering alone does not indicate hypothermia, but it does indicate that the body is having a problem with cold stress.

Symptoms and Treatment

3-47. Mild hypothermia exhibits one or more symptoms: confusion, sleepiness, slurred speech, shallow breathing, weak pulse, change in behavior or appearance, intense shivering, stiffness in the arms or legs, poor control over body movements, slow reactions, and abnormal heart rhythms (usually at the lower end of the 90 °F to 95 °F [32 °C to 35 °C] temperature scale).

3-48. If they notice these symptoms, Soldiers and Marines must take steps to prevent hypothermia from setting in:
- Exchange wet clothing for dry, insulated clothing.
- Conduct physical exercise.
- Hydrate with warm liquids.
- Add heat. To add heat, individuals can go into a shelter, get into a sleeping bag, wrap themselves in blankets, or do a combination of the actions.

3-49. Treatment of mild hypothermia includes the steps mentioned in paragraph 3-42. In all circumstances, the unit must evacuate the individual to a medical facility for treatment. Medical personnel need to monitor the heart. If medical personnel detect abnormal heart rhythms, they must deter the patient from exercising or assisting in the evacuation. Instead, medical personnel prepare the patient for litter evacuation to a medical facility.

3-50. Moderate and severe hypothermia symptoms include dilated pupils, lack of shivering, low blood pressure, unconsciousness, and absent or abnormal heart rhythms. As the core body temperature continues to fall, it may be difficult or impossible to detect signs of life. Medical personnel have revived victims of hypothermia with core temperatures as low as 60 °F (16 °C). Hence, the adage in the medical community, "A person is not dead until they are warm and dead."

3-51. Treatment of moderate or severe hypothermia requires immediate hospitalization. There is a high risk for heart failure. Rescuers should carefully prepare the casualty for litter evacuation (gently placed in a sleeping bag on a sleeping pad or equivalent, then into litter). Rescuers ensure that the casualty remains quiet and supine, that they do not jar or move the patient suddenly, and that the casualty does not assist in the evacuation. For prolonged litter evacuations, a full body-vapor barrier system may be appropriate to help mitigate the effects of hypothermia. Rescuers can use the Blizzard Protection System or a field expedient method.

Prevention

3-52. Soldiers and Marines can prevent hypothermia by—

- Using cold weather clothing and equipment properly.
- Staying hydrated.
- Using rest cycles adequately.
- Eating hot meals.
- Using warming shelters.

3-53. Warming shelters can mean the difference between success and failure in cold region environments. Units anticipate the need for warming shelters for personnel. These shelters enable Soldiers and Marines to eat, drink, rest, conduct personal hygiene, and dry and maintain clothing and equipment while protected from the elements.

Chilblain

3-54. Chilblain (also known as pernio or kibe) is a nonfreezing cold injury. Typically it occurs after 1 to 5 hours in cold-wet conditions at temperatures below 50 °F (10 °C). Small lesions appear on the skin usually on the tops of the fingers. Ears, face, and exposed shins may also show lesions. The lesions are swollen, tender, itchy, and painful. Upon re-warming, the skin becomes inflamed, red, hot to the touch, and swollen. Often, an itching or burning sensation continues for several hours after exposure. Eventually all symptoms subside. There are no lasting effects from chilblain. Units treat chilblain by moving the individual to a warming shelter. Wearing issued clothing properly along with staying adequately hydrated and nourished should prevent chilblain. Soldiers refer to table 4-8 in TB MED 508 for recovery information. Marines refer to MCRP 3-35.1A.

Frostbite

3-55. Frostbite is frozen body tissue. The ambient air temperature must be below 32 °F (0 °C) for this injury to occur. If the ambient temperature is above 32 °F (0 °C), but is below 32 °F (0 °C) with wind chill, frostbite cannot occur. Frostbite generally occurs to exposed skin or extremities such as the nose, ears, cheeks, hands, and feet. Contact frostbite can occur when bare skin is cooled quickly from contact with an extremely cold object. Frostbite can also occur instantaneously when skin comes in contact with super-cooled liquids that do not freeze at 32 °F (0 °C). These products include gasoline, petroleum products, antifreeze, and alcohol (to include alcohol-based wipes). The level of tissue involvement defines each of the four degrees of frostbite. Only a medical doctor can diagnose the degree of frostbite. **For field diagnosis and treatment, frostbite can be classified as superficial or deep.**

Types of Frostbite

3-56. The first sign of frostbite is numbness. As skin cools, individuals feel an uncomfortable sensation of cold, which often includes tingling, burning, aching, sharp pain, and decreased sensation. These symptoms are replaced by numbness as the skin continues to cool and then freezes.

3-57. In **superficial frostbite**, Soldiers and Marines often note that the affected area feels "wooden." The skin initially turns red. Later it becomes pale gray or waxy white. In dark skinned individuals, the skin often remains red. The affected skin moves freely over pliable underlying layers.

3-58. In **deep frostbite**, the skin is cold and firm to the touch. The skin will not move over underlying layers. At a minimum, the affected area includes the upper layers of skin and can include all tissues down to and including the bone.

3-59. A field expedient method to test for superficial or deep frostbite is to use the rebound method. Individuals push on the frostbite area and if the skin returns to its normal position after pressure is removed then the frostbite is superficial. While this method is good for initial diagnosis, Soldiers and Marines must always consult medical personnel if they suspect frostbite.

Treatment of Frostbite

3-60. Professionals in a medical facility must evaluate all frostbite cases. Treatment in the field depends on the treatment of other injuries, the possibility of hypothermia, the possibility of re-freezing, and the ease of evacuation. Medics must consider and treat hypothermia or other potentially life-threatening injuries first. In most cases during field training, Soldiers and Marines will have access to a warming shelter. For superficial frostbite, the affected area can be re-warmed at room temperature or with skin-to-skin contact. Techniques include covering cheeks or nose with warm hands, placing uncovered fingers under opposite armpits, and placing bare feet against the belly of a companion. For deep frostbite, rescuers must move the patient to a warm shelter and keep the patient warm for the duration of the evacuation to a hospital. The injury can be re-warmed using the same techniques or using the warm water bath technique described in paragraph 3-63.

3-61. Additionally, rescuers must insulate and protect thawed injuries from re-freezing during evacuation. Once a tissue has thawed, it must never re-freeze. Thawing and then re-freezing the injury causes additional damage. If there is a chance that the tissue will thaw and then re-freeze (for example, during evacuation), rescuers must keep the injury frozen and *not* thaw the injury.

3-62. Rescuers touch areas with frostbite with care. They avoid rubbing, massaging, or bending the affected areas. They do not rub the affected area with snow or ice and do not use cold-water baths. If transportation is available, casualties avoid walking on frozen feet. If they must walk, it will be better to keep the feet frozen during evacuation.

3-63. Re-warming of frostbite requires skill and care. If medics decide to re-warm the frostbite injury, they prepare a warm water bath between 98 °F and 104 °F (37 °C and 40 °C). They require a container and thermometer. The container must be large enough to accommodate the frostbitten tissue without the tissue touching the sides or bottom of the container. Medics never use hot water as it could cause additional tissue damage. They use a thermometer that reads in the range of 98 °F to 104 °F (37 °C to 40 °C). They gently circulate the water around the affected tissue. They avoid using excessive heat sources such as engine exhaust, open flames, stovetops, heat packs, or steam to thaw an injury. Re-warming of deep frostbite injuries may produce the appearance of blisters known as blebs. Leave the blebs intact. If a bleb ruptures, treat it with a topical antibiotic and cover it with a sterile bandage.

3-64. Casualties must avoid tobacco products when receiving treatment for frostbite. Tobacco products reduce the flow of blood to extremities.

Prevention of Frostbite

3-65. The prevention methods for frostbite mirror those for hypothermia. Soldiers and Marines may not even be aware that they are developing frostbite, especially on the face. Buddy teams must watch each other closely for signs and symptoms of frostbite and take action if they notice frostbite. Prevention also includes the following:

- Always use contact gloves to handle equipment. Never allow bare hands to come in contact with equipment. Always use approved gloves to handle fuel and products made from petroleum, oil, and lubricants.
- Avoid tight fitting clothing and boots. Any interference with the circulation of blood increases the risk of frostbite. Proper sizing of clothing and boots is a critical function that must be taken care of at issue facilities.
- Avoid tobacco products.
- Cover all exposed skin when the wind chill danger is high.

Snow Blindness

3-66. Snow blindness is burning of the cornea of the eye by exposure of the eyes to intense ultraviolet rays of the sun in a snow-covered environment. Snow blindness can occur even when clouds diffuse the sun. Symptoms include severe eye pain, pink or red eyes, and extreme sensitivity to light.

3-67. To treat this injury, loosely bandage the individual's eyes with sterile gauze. Rest is prescribed for at least 36 and up to 72 hours. Since essentially blind while healing from snow blindness, individuals will need constant care in the field to accomplish even routine tasks. Individuals can manage pain with over-the-counter pain medications. Soldiers and Marines can easily prevent this injury by wearing sunglasses or tinted goggles (preferably with ultraviolet protection).

CLOTHING

3-68. A cold weather uniform must accomplish four functions: keep the user functional down to ambient temperatures of -60 °F (-51 °C) (with moderate movement), keep the user dry, protect the user from wind, and provide adequate ventilation. The Army's cold weather uniform system—the Extended Cold Weather Clothing System (ECWCS)—is designed to accomplish these four goals. The Marine Corps uses the same system but refers to it as the mountain cold weather clothing system (known as MCWCS). This manual uses the term ECWCS to refer to both systems. Both systems are constructed by applying three key principles:

- Insulate.
- Layer.
- Ventilate.

3-69. The ECWCS provides insulation to reduce the amount of heat lost to the environment. Several loose layers work better than one heavy garment. The layers of the ECWCS produce greater insulation and adjustability. Air space provides the insulation qualities. Ventilation helps control the amount of heat retained or lost. Excess heat produces perspiration that soaks the clothing and raises the potential for cold injuries.

Extended/Mountain (USMC) Cold Weather Clothing System

3-70. There are two versions of ECWCS issued to Soldiers: Generation II ECWCS and Generation III ECWCS. Marines refer to MCRP 3-35.1A for cold weather clothing systems. Both versions consist of three basic layers:

- Base layer (vapor transmission layer).
- Insulation layer.
- Outer shell layer (protective layer).

3-71. The base layers (also known as inner or wicking layers) lay adjacent to the body. They should fit comfortably loose. These garments wick excess moisture away from the body.

3-72. The insulation layers are the intermediate layers. They provide volume to trap warm air between the body and the outer garments. In addition, the insulation layers help wick away excess moisture. These layers should fit comfortably loose to trap a sufficient volume of air.

3-73. The outer shell layer provides protection from precipitation and wind. In addition, they provide additional volume for trapping warm air. These layers should also fit comfortably loose.

3-74. The acronym COLD-R means clean, overheating, loose and layered, dry, and repair and replace. It defines the principles for the most effective use of ECWCS and other garments for old regions.

3-75. **Keep it clean**. Clothing keeps individuals warm by trapping warm air against the body and in the spaces of the clothing itself. If these spaces become filled with dirt, sweat, body oils, or other grime, the clothing will not perform efficiently. Therefore, individuals must keep clothes as clean as possible so they can stay as warm as possible. When washing is not possible, Soldiers and Marines can dry rub and air clothing.

3-76. **Avoid overheating**. The key is not for the user to be hot, but comfortably cool. Profuse sweating indicates that the individual overdressed. Soldiers and Marines must exhibit personal discipline to adjust or remove clothing to prevent overheating. When determining uniform standards, leaders—rather than becoming too restrictive—determine only the outer garment of the uniform. Personnel can then shed other inner garments depending on how they feel. Since individuals handle the cold differently (see paragraphs 3-21 through 3-37), no one set uniform can be dictated; however, units can establish a general range.

3-77. Leaders conduct pre-combat inspections to ensure that Soldiers and Marines do not overdress before starting movement. Often, they don every available piece of cold weather uniform to establish the "warm" feeling. This will cause them to sweat when they start movement. If they do become cold when moving, they have nothing left to wear that will compensate for the low temperature. Appendix A includes a general uniform guide that will help leaders, Soldiers, and Marines in determining the appropriate uniform for various temperature ranges.

3-78. **Wear clothes loose and layered**. Loose, layered clothing creates pockets of warm air. The more layers used, the more warm air will be trapped. Tight clothing prevents air from becoming trapped between the body and clothes. Several thin layers working together work better than one thick layer alone.

3-79. **Keep clothing dry**. Moisture enters clothing from two directions: inside-perspiration and outside-precipitation (such as rain, snow, ice, and frost). Moisture reduces insulating properties of clothing. Once clothing is wet, the water or sweat evaporates, drawing warmth away from the body. Before entering heated shelters, personnel brush off snow or ice to prevent it from melting and soaking clothes. If damp, clothing dries best inside heated shelters away from direct heat. Leather items should be dried slowly. Turn windproof or waterproof breathable parka clothing inside-out to facilitate drying in a heated shelter.

3-80. **Repair and replace**. Soldiers and Marines repair damaged clothing and replace nonrepairable or nonfunctioning gear. They must constantly inspect their clothing for serviceability and repair or replace items as necessary.

Generation II ECWCS

3-81. The base layer consists of a polypropylene undershirt and drawers with standard wool socks. This set of clothing is commonly referred to as polypro. (See left side of figure 3-1.) Soldiers wear the polypro next to their skin. They DO NOT wear cotton undergarments under the polypro. They DO NOT wear Army combat uniforms (ACUs) on top of the base layer in the field. Cotton absorbs and traps moisture. Instead, Soldiers wear nylon shorts as an alternative to cotton underwear. Women wear a nylon sports bra. The issued polypro layer has a zipper to form a mock turtleneck or to ventilate as the workload increases. Soldiers can layer the lightweight, midweight, and heavyweight versions of polypro. This allows them more flexibility to remove garments as the workload increases. For more effective wicking, they can wear the nylon dress sock or a polypro liner sock under the wool sock. An arctic necklace consists of 550-foot (168-meter) cord with a lighter and lip balm worn next to the body. Wearing this necklace allows Soldiers to keep the lighter warm and nearby and lip balm pliable. Marines refer to MCRP 3-35.1A for how to wear cold weather clothing systems.

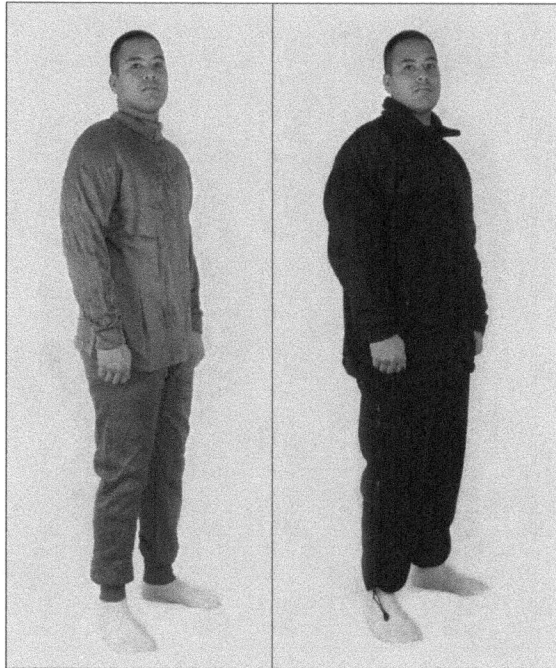

Figure 3-1. Generation II ECWCS base layer and polar fleece top and bottom

3-82. The insulation layer consists of—

- Black fleece shirt and overalls.
- Liners cold weather coat and trousers.

3-83. Black fleece shirt and overalls (commonly referred to as polar fleece top and bottom) appears on the right side of figure 3-1. Some individuals receive the black fleece layer for ECWCS. They wear the polar fleece over the base layer. The shirt has a "pit zips" for ventilation. Personnel can use the full-length zipper to form a mock turtleneck or to open the shirt for ventilation. By tightly cinching the drawstring at the bottom, they can keep wind from coming up under the shirt. The bibs are also sized short intentionally. The full-length zippers on each pant leg allow personnel to don and remove the bibs without removing their boots. The Army has approved the use of this garment as an outer shell layer. However, it offers little protection from the wind and no protection from moisture.

3-84. Liners cold weather coat and trousers (commonly referred to as smoking jacket and pants) appears on the left side of figure 3-2. The cold weather coat and trouser liner for the ECWCS is made from the same material as the poncho liner—1-ounce rip stop nylon quilted over polyester batting. Personnel wear this item over the base layer. The coat has slits under the arms for ventilation. The trousers are sized short intentionally to avoid the need to tuck them into the boot.

Figure 3-2. Generation II ECWCS liners cold weather coat and trousers and outer layer

3-85. The outer layer consists of the Generation II ECWCS windproof and waterproof breathable parka (see the right side of figure 3-2). Units issue these in woodland camouflage, desert camouflage, or the universal camouflage patterns, as in the ACU. The parka does not have an inner liner. It has hand-warmer and cargo pockets at the waist as well as two map pockets adjacent to the zipper and two sleeve pockets. Troops can store the hood away but cannot attach a fur ruff. This parka has a snow skirt to prevent snow and wind from entering underneath the jacket and "pit zips" for ventilation. The trousers have two hand warmer pockets and two cargo pockets. Suspenders are issued separately. Personnel wear suspenders with the X pattern centered between the shoulder blades. They wear the metal hook so that the piece of fabric sits against the body to prevent the metal hook from rubbing on the skin.

3-86. Units also issue balaclavas that personnel can wear in three configurations: a hat, a head cover, and a face cover. To wear as a hat, individuals fold the bottom of the balaclava to the inside to form a hat. They place the hat onto their head with the face opening to the rear. Condensation from their breathing forms on their forehead. If they need to change configurations later, this will prevent them from placing wet material onto their face. To wear as a head cover, individuals wear the balaclava down, exposing their face. They pull the balaclava over their head and pull the lower portion of the face opening under their chin. To wear as a face cover, individuals wear the balaclava down, face covered. They pull the lower portion of the face opening up over their mouth and nose. They use goggles to cover eyes and remaining exposed skin if required.

3-87. Intermediate cold-wet boots with removable liners (tan) are rated from 68 °F to 14 °F (20 °C to -10 °C). Personnel should receive two pairs of liners with this boot. Army combat boots (hot weather) are not acceptable for cold region environments. Army combat boots (temperate weather) are acceptable until the temperature drops below 32 °F (0 °C).

3-88. Extended cold weather boots are also known as white vapor barrier (VB) boots or bunny boots. They are rated 14 °F to -60 °F (-10 °C to -51 °C) and are for use in cold dry environments. Some VB boots have a pressure relief valve. Soldiers and Marines use the valve for airborne operations. When they change altitude rapidly, they open the valve briefly to equalize pressure and then close the valve. For all other operations, personnel keep the valve closed to prevent moisture from entering the boot. At least once daily, personnel wipe VB boots out and change socks at the same time. Soldiers and Marines use black VB boots, rated to -20 °F (-29 °C), in cold wet environments.

3-89. Soldiers and Marines switch to VB boots when temperatures range from 14 °F to -19 °F (-10 °C to -28 °C). When Soldiers and Marines switch depends on the workload. Leaders should ensure that personnel have both pairs of boots available in the event of a temperature swing or change of mission. This will give maximum flexibility.

3-90. Soldiers and Marines can wear the neck gaiter in three configurations. First, they can wear the neck gaiter around the neck as a turtleneck. Second, they can wear it pulled up over the head with the face exposed. Third, they can extend the second configuration by pulling the bottom of the gaiter up over the mouth and nose.

3-91. At a minimum, individuals always wear a contact glove when working in the cold. A contact glove is a lightweight glove that affords the user some dexterity. Contact gloves protect users from getting their skin stuck to an object by directly touching it. They must always have a layer that separates their skin from a cold object.

3-92. The leather windproof and waterproof breathable, lined gloves with the wool inserts work best. The inserts serve as a contact glove. Units issue Soldiers and Marines two pairs of wool inserts. The trigger finger mittens are made of canvas and deer skin palms (this skin maintains flexibility in cold). Individuals wear the trigger finger mittens with the wool trigger finger inserts. The arctic mittens are made of canvas with deer skin palms and polyester fiber backing that serves as a face warmer. They have a removable liner made from the same material as the poncho liner. Personnel need to pull the liners out and inspect for holes, especially near any seams. Both the trigger finger mittens and arctic mittens have lanyards that allow removing the mittens without losing them. Individuals wear the lanyard over their head. If not wearing the mittens, Soldiers and Marines tuck them inside the outer shell of their parka to keep out snow and to keep them warm for later use. Leaders keep routine tasks routine by rehearsing with mittens.

Note: Fuels do not freeze and will be the same temperature as the air. To prevent frostbite, Soldiers and Marines **always** wear gloves designed for handling petroleum products when working with fuels.

3-93. Soldiers and Marines dry out clothing as soon as possible. Then, they can re-use an item when needed. Personnel can wear damp clothing items close to the body (between the inner and intermediate layer) to dry or place the items in the sleeping bag to dry out overnight. Larger items that have become wet should not be placed in the sleeping bag. Instead, personnel place them between the sleeping bag and sleeping mat or on drying lines in a heated tent.

3-94. The modular sleep system is designed for a temperature range of 50 °F to -40 °F (10 °C to -40 °C). At the low end of this range, individuals will only stay comfortable for about four hours of sleep. As they sleep, they compress the sleeping bag material causing it to lose its insulating properties. If needed, individuals exit the bag and shake it to restore the insulating properties. Individuals should fluff it before entering.

3-95. Units use the patrol bag (green with foliage green) when temperatures stay above 30 °F (-1 °C). If personnel do not have a shelter, they use the patrol bag with the bivouac cover. They use the intermediate cold weather bag (black or gray-green) when temperatures fluctuate from 30 °F to -10 °F (-1 °C to -23 °C). In temperatures below -10 °F (-23 °C), personnel insert the black or gray-green bag into the green bag and snap and zip them together. The double bag works inside the patrol base cover for a temperature rating of -40 °F (-40 °C). The newer ACU has a bag style rated to -45 °F (-43 °C). Soldiers and Marines should wear no more than a single base layer inside the bag. They should not sweat inside the bag.

3-96. The thick polyethylene foam pad puts insulation between the individual and the ground. This insulating layer is essential to the sleep system as it prevents conductive heat loss to the ground. If personnel lose or destroy the sleeping pad, they can use pine boughs, cardboard, or other such materials as an insulating layer.

Generation III ECWCS

3-97. Generation III ECWCS is a seven layer clothing system currently fielded across the Army. Slightly different versions have been fielded, so slight uniform differences might occur. Generation III ECWCS uses the same four principles as Generation II ECWCS, but this system utilizes seven layers instead of the three layers utilized by Generation II ECWCS. Marines refer to MCRP 3-35.1A.

Layer 1: Lightweight Cold Weather Undershirt and Drawers

3-98. The lightweight cold weather undershirt and drawers include a long-sleeve top and full-length bottom garments constructed out of silk-weight moisture wicking polyester. (See the left side of figure 3-3.) The material helps move moisture from the skin to the outer layers both while the wearer is moving or static. The top has holes in the sleeves for the thumbs. By placing thumbs through the holes, Soldiers keep the garment down around their wrists. They wear these items next to skin or with the midweight cold weather shirt and drawers to add insulation and to aid the transfer of moisture.

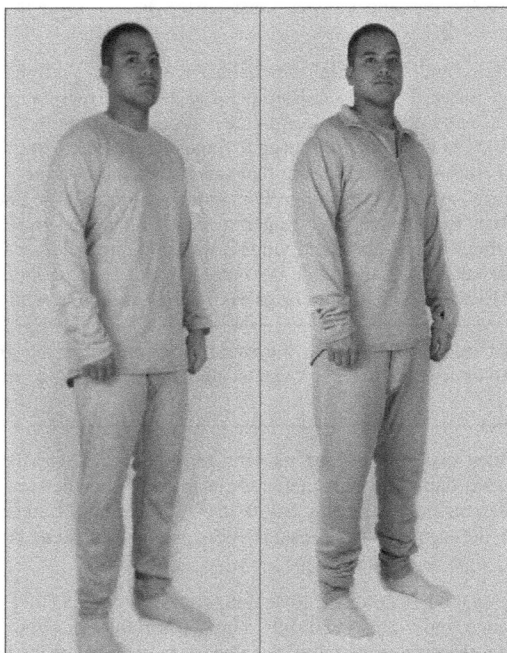

Figure 3-3. Generation III ECWCS layers 1 and 2

Layer 2: Midweight Cold Weather Shirt and Drawers

3-99. The midweight cold weather shirt and drawers consist of a long-sleeve top and full-length bottom garments constructed out of polyester grid fleece. (See the right side of figure 3-3.) This material provides light insulation for use in mild climates and a layer of insulation for colder climates. The top has a zipper that can form a mock turtleneck or open to ventilate as workload increases. The top has holes in the sleeves for the thumbs. By placing thumbs through the holes, Soldiers keep the garment down around their wrists. They wear this layer over lightweight cold weather undershirt and drawers or next to skin.

Layer 3: The Fleece Jacket

3-100. The fleece jacket acts as the primary insulation layer for use in moderate to cold climates. (See the left side of figure 3-4.) The fleece mimics animal fur and provides an increase in the warmth-to-weight ratio along with a reduction in volume when packed. The jacket has two inner mesh pockets. The zipper closes to form a mock turtleneck or opens for ventilation. Soldiers wear the jacket underneath shell layers. The Army approved this layer for use as an outer layer. However, the fleece jacket offers little protection from wind and no protection from moisture. It is recommended that Soldiers use this jacket with a shell layer only.

Figure 3-4. Generation III ECWCS layers 3 and 4

Layer 4: The Wind Cold Weather Jacket

3-101. The wind cold weather jacket is made of a lightweight, windproof, and water repellant material. (See the right side of figure 3-4.) It acts as a minimum outer shell layer, improving the performance of moisture wicking of the insulation layers when combined with body armor, ACUs, or both. It has two sleeve pockets and a mock turtleneck. Two chest level pockets with mesh pocket linings aid in ventilation while wearing body armor. Soldiers wear this jacket as wind protection during windy cool days.

Layer 5: The Soft Shell Cold Weather Jacket and Trousers Outer Shell Layer

3-102. The soft shell cold weather jacket and trousers outer shell layer are made of a highly water resistant, windproof material that increases moisture vapor transfer over current hard shell garments. (See the left side of figure 3-5 on page 3-18.) This layer reduces weight, bulk, and the noise signature during movement. The increase of breathability improves performance of insulation layers by decreasing saturation due to moisture accumulation. The jacket has a storable hood that works with the ballistic helmet. It has two hand warming pockets on the chest with mesh lining and pit zips to aid in ventilation. It has two sleeve pockets. It has draw cords on the bottom to prevent snow and wind from entering the system. Soldiers wear this layer when the average temperature falls below 14 °F (-10 °C). Soldiers determine the base and insulation layers necessary from the temperature, wind, and activity level.

Figure 3-5. Generation III ECWCS layers 5, 6 and 7

Layer 6: The Extended Cold/Wet Weather Jacket and Trousers

3-103.   The extended cold wet weather jacket and trousers are the waterproof layer for use in prolonged or hard rain and cold wet conditions. (See the middle picture of figure 3-5.) The jacket has two pass-through chest pockets for ventilation and a storable hood that works with the ballistic helmet. Soldiers wear this layer when the average temperature is above 14 °F (-10 °C) and alternating between freezing and thawing. They determine the base and insulation layers necessary from the temperature, wind, and activity level.

Layer 7: The Extended Cold Weather Parka and Trousers

3-104.   The extended cold weather parka and trousers provide superior warmth with high compact ability, low weight, and low volume. (See the right side of figure 3-5.) With highly water resistant and windproof fabric, it provides wind and moisture protection. It is sized to fit over the body armor during movement or static activities requiring maximum insulation. Trouser design incorporates full side zippers for donning and doffing over boots and other layers. Soldiers wear this layer in extreme cold regions and climates over all other layers. It is the last layer of protection. It is meant for static positions.

WEAPONS CONSIDERATIONS

3-105.   Cold weather adversely affects all weapons, the lubricants used to maintain weapons, and ammunition. Soldiers and Marines must understand and take steps to reduce these effects to keep their weapons working in a cold region environment. Paragraphs 3-106 through 3-133 describe the effects of extreme cold regions on weapons and describe techniques for ensuring weapons function in the cold region environment.

GENERAL CLIMATIC EFFECTS ON WEAPONS SYSTEMS

3-106. Weapon systems encounter common problems in cold region environments. Units should consult FM 9-207 and applicable technical manuals for a more detailed listing of technical issues that weapons experience in cold regions.

Sluggishness

3-107. Weapons function under extreme cold conditions if given proper care. Lubricants that personnel normally use under temperate conditions—such as cleaning, lubricating, and preservative compound (CLP)—thicken in cold regions and stoppages or sluggish weapon action will result from their use. CLP will freeze at -35 °F (-37 °C). To eliminate this problem, individuals must strip the weapon completely, thoroughly clean it, and lubricate it with lubricating oil arctic, weapons (LAW). At a minimum, they should lightly oil the camming surfaces of the bolt with LAW. They can leave the rest of the weapon dry. LAW is available in one-quart containers but not in the refillable half-ounce bottles normally found in weapons cleaning kits. If Soldiers and Marines do not have LAW available, they use a dry graphite lubricant or fire the weapon dry.

Condensation

3-108. Condensation forms on weapons when personnel move them from the cold into a warmer environment. This is called sweating. If personnel return weapons to the cold without removing the condensation, this sweat can turn to ice, which will result in stoppages. For this reason, personnel should leave weapons outside when temperatures are below freezing. When left outside, weapons should be readily accessible but sheltered. Shelter prevents ice and snow from getting into the working parts of the weapon (such as the sights and barrel). If necessary, Soldiers and Marines can take weapons inside for cleaning. Weapons will continue to sweat for approximately one hour after coming into a warm shelter. Individuals must wait until the sweating process stops before thoroughly cleaning their weapons. If units keep weapons in heated shelters, Soldiers and Marines should keep weapons near, but not on, the floor to minimize condensation.

Fouling from Snow and Ice

3-109. To keep snow and ice out of a weapon, it needs some type of cover. Soldiers and Marines should request muzzle caps from the unit armorer. Such caps are expendable and will do the job. If none are available, individuals improvise. They can use plastic bags, tape, or condoms. Soldiers and Marines close ejection port covers. Personnel should carry something to de-ice a weapon if part of the weapon becomes frozen. Windshield wiper fluid carried in a small bottle works as does aircraft de-icer and antifreeze. Periodic cycling of the weapon will also keep parts from freezing. Soldiers and Marines operate the action on weapons periodically. This can help identify icing issues.

Visibility Issues

3-110. Soldiers and Marines can encounter a visibility problem when they fire weapons in still air conditions with temperatures below -30 °F (-34 °C). As the round leaves the weapon, the hot propellant gases cause the water vapor in the air to condense. These droplets of condensed water vapor then freeze, creating ice particles that produce a cloud of ice fog. This fog will hang over the weapon and follow the path of the projectile, obstructing the gunner's vision along the line of fire as well as revealing the gunner's location to the enemy. When faced with this problem, fire at a slower rate and/or relocate to an alternate firing position. Tests have shown that even in warmer temperatures, a fog develops around the gun. Hot gases from the gun and the breath of the gunner create the fog, making it difficult for the gunner to observe the strike of rounds. For crew-served weapons, the assistant gunner may need to take up a position further left or right to help with adjustments. For individual weapons, Soldiers and Marines may need to change position frequently. When using optics in the cold, gunners must avoid breathing on the sight. Breathing on the sight causes condensation. Since the warmth put out by the proximity of the face can cloud the sight, individuals allow a space between the eye and the sight. When taken from a cold to a warm environment, individuals allow the optics to adjust to the new temperature slowly to avoid cracking the lens.

Breakage and Malfunctions

3-111. Extreme cold causes metal and plastic to become more brittle than it is at warmer temperatures. Breakage generally occurs early when individuals fire a cold weapon. When fired, the metal heats and rapid, unequal expansion of parts occurs. They should begin firing small arms at a slow rate of fire in extreme cold regions, if the tactical situation permits. The slower rate of fire greatly reduces potential weapon malfunctioning. Freezing of moisture produced by sweating or accumulated snow or ice in the weapon will also cause malfunctions and stoppages. After firing a weapon, the heat it has generated can cause any snow or ice it touches to melt. This water will then re-freeze and may cause the weapon to malfunction. Soldiers and Marines can use a de-icer to thaw the weapon and keep it working properly. They can also cycle the weapon periodically. Unit armorers need to carry extra parts to overcome these problems.

3-112. Automatic weapons have a high rate of breakage and malfunction in a cold region environment. Especially affected are the sear and bolt parts. Gun crews must carry extra parts of this type. One common malfunction is short recoil where the bolt does not recoil fully to the rear. A second malfunction is caused by the freezing and hardening of buffers. This causes great shock and rapid recoil, increasing cyclic rate and can cause parts to break. Soldiers and Marines must coat all internal components and friction surfaces of machine-guns with LAW. If personnel do not have LAW available, they should fire these small arms cold and dry. They begin firing slowly at first to allow the weapon to warm; they use short, two- or three-round bursts at short intervals until the weapon components warm. Soldiers and Marines test fire machine-guns in cold regions prior to combat deployment to a cold region area of operations. They transport ammunition in enclosed drums or cans to prevent snow fouling. They keep the ammunition at the same temperature as the weapons.

Emplacement Issues

3-113. Crew-served weapons require some type of base or platform for firing. Emplacement of a weapon on snow, ice, or frozen ground may result in a broken weapon, inaccurate firing due to sinking, or the inability to absorb shock. Paragraphs 3-115 through 3-133 discuss emplacements relating to particular weapons.

Reduced Velocity and Range of Projectiles

3-114. Soldiers and Marines need to re-zero all weapons in when deploying to cold regions. As temperature drops, so does the muzzle velocity, and thus the range of projectiles. The range changes because internal and external ballistics change. Internal ballistics occur inside the weapon. As the burning rate of propellant decreases, the rate of gas expansion decreases, and the rate at which the projectile moves down the barrel decreases. External ballistics occur after the projectile leaves the muzzle. Decreased muzzle velocity reduces the stability of the projectile as it leaves the muzzle, possibly causing the projectile to tumble. At longer ranges, this further reduces velocity and accuracy. Colder air is denser than warmer air and may create increased drag on the projectile thus further decreasing range.

CONSIDERATIONS FOR SPECIFIC WEAPONS SYSTEMS

3-115. This section covers issues that common weapon systems have when operated in the cold region environment. FM 9-207 and applicable technical manuals provide a more detailed list. Marines also reference MCRP 3-35.1A.

9mm Pistol

3-116. The 9mm pistol is a reliable weapon. Rarely do its moving parts break, but some breakage of the extractor and the firing pin can occur. Condensation affects this weapon more than other weapons. Often, personnel whose duties require them to frequently enter and exit heated shelters and vehicles carry it. Sluggishness and condensation are common problems. Freezing generally occurs around the slide and magazine well.

M16A2/M4 Rifle

3-117.   Little breakage will occur if individuals fire the M16A2/M4 rifle at a slow rate of fire until warm. Breakage usually occurs around the extractor, ejector, and firing pin. Condensation in the buffer tube will decrease the shock absorbing ability, which may result in breakage or reduced recoil, which can result in the omission of the cocking step in the cycle of operation. To remove condensation and reduce the chance of having the weapon malfunction, Soldiers and Marines frequently wipe the buffer tube out. They also re-zero the weapon when deploying from a temperate to a cold environment. Cold temperatures may cause a decrease in the burning rate of propellants, which can significantly change projectile trajectories. In effect, this will nullify the zero of the weapon. Altitude also affects a weapon system, and when a significant change in altitude occurs, the weapon should also be re-zeroed. When individuals wear mittens or bulky hand wear, they open the trigger guide for firing. When not in use, Soldiers and Marines keep the trigger guard closed but unlatched for safety.

M249 Squad Automatic Weapon

3-118.   The M249 squad automatic weapon has a high rate of breakage due to the large number of moving parts. Armorers should carry plenty of spare parts, especially those most prone to failure (firing pins, extractors, and feed pawls). The M249 safety selector switch is extremely difficult to operate when the weapon is cold soaked. The cold region environment affects buffer group assemblies in the same manner as the M16/M4 (see paragraph 3-117). A common malfunction is short recoil (bolt does not recoil fully to the rear) that occurs early in firing. Apply immediate action procedures until the metal warms. When changing barrels, personnel avoid placing a hot barrel in the snow. The rapid cooling of the barrel may warp it and will cause condensation to freeze in the barrel. Soldiers and Marines protect the ammunition since unprotected belts can introduce ice into the weapon when firing. Personnel can construct semi-permanent platforms by attaching ski pole baskets or snowshoes to the bipod. Ski pole baskets only work well in hard or compacted snow; issuing an extra snowshoe without bindings to weapons crews works best.

M240 Machine Gun

3-119.   The same considerations as the M16/M249 apply to the M240 machine gun. Emplacement considerations may be more involved. For the bipod, individuals apply the same techniques mentioned for the M249 (ski baskets or snowshoes). Testing has shown that resting the weapon on a rucksack fails to provide a stable platform and makes it difficult to operate from the kneeling (too low) or the prone position (too high). For the tripod, personnel might use the ahkio as a platform (see paragraphs 2-42 and 3-147 for more details on the ahkio). On hard ground or ice, the base of each leg of the tripod sits in a slot that is chipped out to fit it. Ice screws or pitons driven into frozen ground or ice and attached to the tripod legs with 550-cord may increase the stability of the position.

M2 Heavy Machine Gun

3-120.   The same considerations as the M16/M249 apply to the M2 heavy machine gun. For the tripod, see the techniques noted for the M240 in paragraph 3-119. Soldiers and Marines have also used sandbags to provide a stable platform for the tripod on hard ground, but tests have shown the bags to rip after 300 to 400 rounds.

MK-19 Automatic Grenade Launcher

3-121.   The MK-19 automatic grenade launcher requires grease, molybdenum disulfide (known as GMD) lubricant when used at low temperatures. Cloth covers work better than plastics to protect the weapon from the elements. Plastic or rubberized covers can become stiff or brittle in the cold. This may result in difficulty removing (especially when in a hurry) or damaging the cover. For the tripod, see the techniques noted for the M240 machine gun in paragraph 3-119.

Mortars

3-122.   When using mortars in a cold region environment, Soldiers and Marines consider the effects on their hands, the mortar ballistic computer, emplacement of aiming stakes and base plates, and malfunctions induced by the cold.

3-123.   Soldiers and Marines must always wear hand protection (contact gloves). The gloves must not be loose; they must fit snuggly to prevent a hazard. When dropping the ammunition into the tube, the tube's vacuum can suck a loose glove into the tube. Paragraph 3-91 gives more information on contact gloves.

3-124.   Units program the mortar ballistic computer to accept temperatures down to -50 °F (-46 °C). This automatically compensates for cold-induced slow burning of charges when computing firing data. The mortar ballistic computer is not programmed for temperature inputs colder than -50 °F (-46 °C). Breathing on sights or on the mortar ballistic computer will fog and freeze equipment.

3-125.   Aiming stakes for mortars become loose when placed in snow. Soldiers and Marines use sandbags or anchoring devices to keep mortars in place once set. Base plates become brittle when exposed to extreme cold. This, coupled with the decreased ability of frozen ground to absorb shock, results in base plates being more prone to breakage than normal. If possible, troops dig in base plates to prevent plates from skipping. Shock absorbing materials—such as spruce branches, sandbags, even ice chips or soil—absorb recoil during firing. Efficient material works only if it prevents the base plate from bouncing out of its hole. To prepare a firing position quickly, individuals can use demolitions (1.25 pound block of C-4 works well). After emplacement, Soldiers and Marines may find the base plates hard to remove.

3-126.   Mortar malfunctions occur in direct proportion to the severity of the weather. After each mission, Soldiers and Marines swab bores thoroughly to remove any excess propellants. Personnel avoid using point detonating (PD) fuses due to the severe dampening effects of snow. Airbursts are preferred. As temperatures fall, the rubber tube cover may harden and become extremely difficult to remove. When firing in drop mode, expect a greater number of misfires. Using the trigger will correct this in some instances. Soldiers and Marines should cover muzzles and sights when not firing the weapon to prevent snow and ice from entering the tube. Personnel need to check mortar technical manuals for appropriate misfire procedures.

3-127.   The M136 (AT-4) antitank weapon has plastic and rubber components that become brittle and can crack in extreme cold. When personnel fire the weapon, ice fog and vapor trails occur. Sights are more difficult to release from their covers in cold temperatures. To prevent the icing of sights, the gunner wears a facemask or scarf when temperatures reach -15 °F (-26 °C).

M220 Tube-Launched, Optically Tracked, Wire-Guided Missile Weapons System

3-128.   The M220 tube-launched, optically tracked, wire-guided missile (known as TOW) weapon system works effectively in temperatures to -25 °F (-32 °C). Units can store this system in temperatures to -65 °F (-54 °C). Units double the backblast danger and caution area size if the temperature is below 0 °F (-18 °C). In extreme cold, the heat from the engine can distort the image in the sight.

Man-Portable Air Defense System (Stinger)

3-129.   The man-portable air defense system (known as MANPADS), works in colder temperatures with accommodations. Gunners add additional interrogation and tracking time to accommodate temperature-related diminished battery performance. Units must keep the nickel-cadmium battery fully charged. They also double the backblast danger and caution area size if the temperature is below 0 °F (-18 °C).

Javelin Anti-Tank Missile

3-130.   The Javelin anti-tank missile has a slight drop when fired in the cold. When using from defilade or reverse slope positions, gunners must anticipate this drop. Soldiers and Marines can effectively use the Javelin in temperatures to -25 °F (-32 °C). They can store the Javelin in temperatures to -65 °F (-54 °C).

Grenades

3-131. Snow adversely affects grenades. It dissipates the energy from fragmentation grenades reducing the radius that produces casualties. Smoke grenades that sink into the snow and get wet will continue to burn. This burning will melt the snow and create a stain on the ground if the smoke is colored. The optimum solution is to place smoke grenades on a platform in order to maximize performance. Alternatively, personnel can tape or wire a grenade to a stake, forked stick, or solid piece of ice. In extremely cold temperatures the adhesive on tape might not stick.

3-132. Soldiers and Marines take care to ensure grenades do not get stuck to wet gloves while they are being employed. If an individual picks up a cold grenade with a wet glove, often the metal of the grenade will stick to the glove. This creates a hazard for personnel and those around them. A technique to keep the grenade from sticking to the glove is to roll the grenade back and forth in gloved hands prior to pulling the pin to prevent short throws from freezing or sticking to wet gloves.

Demolitions

3-133. In the cold, demolitions have limited uses. The C-4 hardens making it difficult to insert blasting caps. In extreme cold conditions, C-4 has shattered from the blasting cap rather than detonating. Tying the detonation cord is quite difficult in cold temperatures. It often becomes brittle and breaks when individuals try to unroll it. Like other weapon systems, condensation contributes to the incidence of misfires. Gunners compensate for the cold by doubling the hangfire and misfire waiting times.

TACTICAL CONSIDERATIONS

3-134. Soldiers and Marines make tactical considerations in the cold region environment. Tactical considerations involve communications and information systems equipment, acoustic sensors, and shelter requirements. (FM 3-90 discusses general tactical considerations.)

COMMUNICATIONS AND INFORMATION SYSTEMS EQUIPMENT

3-135. Cold temperatures, dry air, condensation, frozen ground, snow, visibility, and electromagnetic conditions adversely affect electronic equipment. Condensation results from rapid temperature changes such as moving from outside to inside. Electronic equipment includes electronic systems, including communication and computers. Any electronic equipment Army forces use must be capable of operating in temperatures to -25 °F (-32 °C). Electronics have special challenges with respect to this requirement and may often require proper heating to above freezing temperatures to operate at all. The Marine Corps has specific communications requirements. See MCWP 3-40.3 for details.

3-136. Most computers and computer displays are not designed to operate at cold temperatures and are generally unavailable for use until warmed. When first turned on, displays appear faint and difficult to read. As the display warms, this improves due to self heating. Most computers in a cold-soaked vehicle are unavailable until the air inside the vehicle has warmed. In general, units need to operate all computer systems in a warmed environment or to pre-heat with individual heaters or devices.

3-137. Communications equipment, including antennas, can be adversely affected by the following:
- Grounding problems.
- Static buildup.
- Noise interference.
- Snow or ice accumulation on antennas.
- Magnetic storms.
- Accuracy of Global Positioning System (GPS).
- Lower temperature limits.

3-138. It often proves difficult to establish an adequate ground for most electronic equipment. It may be impossible to drive grounding rods into the frozen ground. Even if emplaced, the frozen earth has low conductivity and therefore does not provide adequate electrical earth ground. If possible, Soldiers and Marines should install any grounding rods or antennas before the ground freezes. The cold dry air and poor ground conductivity increase the likelihood of static buildup on equipment and personnel. Troops must discharge any static buildup prior to touching electronic equipment.

3-139. Interference created by the cold region environment consists of noise, snow, and solar interferences. Noise interference may result from inadequate ground of other electronic equipment, portable generators, or vehicles. Snow or ice accumulation on antennas and radar systems attenuates signals and interferes with signal propagation.

3-140. Magnetic storms occur in the ionosphere and are associated with solar disturbances (aurora borealis). They can cause severe static, fading, and blackout of radio signals. The degree to which these disturbances affect radio signals depends on the frequency used to transmit the signal. Low frequency (100 to 500 kilohertz) provides the best medium for long distance, point-to-point radio communications. Higher frequency systems use multiple frequencies to allow changing frequencies during a magnetic storm.

3-141. High latitude and cold environments adversely affect the accuracy of GPS. Often fewer GPS satellites exist in such areas. Those that do exist are positioned low on the horizon.

3-142. Most communications and information systems equipment has warmer temperature limits at which they can be operated and stored. To prevent damage to equipment left installed in a cold-soaked vehicle, Soldiers and Marines allow the equipment to come up to operating temperature before turning on the power. In some circumstances, personnel uninstall equipment from vehicles subject to being cold soaked.

ACOUSTIC SENSORS

3-143. Acoustic sensors collect passive or active emitted or reflected sounds, pressure waves, or vibrations in the atmosphere or in water. These sensors detect and track vehicles and personnel. The cold region environment reduces and possibly even nullifies the capabilities of these sensors. Snow—the most absorptive naturally occurring ground cover—causes this reduced performance.

3-144. The properties of the snow further compound the problem of reduced acoustic sensors capabilities. The snow's depth, melt periods, and accompanying wind vary in their effects on acoustic sensors. Snow cover of 1 inch (2 centimeters) in depth is significant enough to cause effects. Soldiers and Marines should search the Cold Regions Research and Engineering Laboratory Web site for the most current information regarding the effects of a cold region environment on acoustic sensors.

SHELTER REQUIREMENTS

3-145. The cold weather presents numerous challenges to individual performance. Normal tasks take longer to accomplish, and Soldiers and Marines need areas where they can heat themselves and recover from the elements to continue mission tasks. Considering the extreme cold found in the cold regions, Soldiers require special shelters and heaters. Appendix B lists the characteristics of both. Marine Corps personnel reference MCRP 3-35.1A for shelter and stove information. As a generalization, many Marine Corps units will not use the equipment in appendix B due to the light nature of the force.

3-146. In cold region environments, the Army uses a tent known as the ten-man arctic tent. Primarily used at the squad level, Soldiers can adapt it for multiple uses. This six-sided pyramidal tent, supported by a center pole, normally accommodates ten Soldiers with their individual equipment. When necessary, it can accommodate additional personnel if they store their equipment outside. Units can also use it as a command post, aid station, or storage shelter. The tent has a liner and two doors, each of which has a series of toggles and loops around their outer edges. When units need additional space, Soldiers use these toggles and loops to join two or more tents together with unrestricted access between them.

3-147. The scow sled, commonly known as the ahkio, has a 200-pound (91 kilogram) capacity. It is the light infantry squad's primary means of transporting tents and other sustainment equipment in a cold region environment. Weighing 38 pounds (17 kilograms), this fiberglass sled has an attached cover. Units also use the ahkio to transport weapons, rations, and ammunition; provide a stable firing platform for crew-served weapons in deep snow; and evacuate casualties. Many units may find that using smaller sleds is desirable. For example, the Marines employ a four-man sled design and do not use the ahkio. There are many designs available for commercial off-the-shelf purchase. Soldiers and Marines can utilize MCRP 3-35.1A for the latest designs on small sleds.

3-148. Not only is tentage important, Soldiers must have a means to produce heat in the cold region environment. Units often use the space heater arctic (SHA) to heat the ten-man arctic tent. The SHA can burn both liquid and solid fuels, although operation with solid fuels requires some minor modification. The SHA and component parts weigh approximately 41 pounds (18.5 kilograms).

3-149. One 5-gallon can of approved liquid fuel burns for approximately 15 hours at the maximum firing rate. Operating temperatures are -60 °F to 50 °F (-51 °C to 10 °C). Operating elevations are 0 to 6,000 feet (1828 meters) above mean sea level. The SHA can operate at higher elevations, but it will require more frequent cleanings and inspections.

3-150. Two potential safety hazards arise when using tents: fuel and poisoning. Soldiers only use approved fuel sources. Gasoline, JP-4, used motor oil, and solvents are examples of fuels that create a fire danger and potential for explosion. Flames can engulf a tent in approximately ten seconds and burn it to the ground in less than a minute.

3-151. The second danger is carbon monoxide poisoning. Carbon monoxide poisoning occurs when individuals breathe fumes from improperly ventilated heat sources. This odorless gas replaces oxygen in the blood stream. Red blood cells actually bind with carbon monoxide more readily than with oxygen; exposure of just a few hours can result in death. Initially symptoms include headache, confusion, tiredness, and excessive yawning. In more severe cases, cherry red lips and unconsciousness precedes cardiac arrest and death.

3-152. Despite these severe safety risks, proper training will do much to mitigate the risk. Additionally, units should always have a fire guard when operating military heaters. Leaders must inspect and ensure these guards are not tired, are fully alert, and have access to a fire extinguisher (5 pound minimum).

3-153. The arctic tent and the SHA are the preferred equipment for operating in a cold region environment. However, many units may lack the time or capability to procure this equipment when they receive deployment notification. In addition to this, certain specialty tents will be required to perform maintenance on tracked and wheeled pieces of equipment.

This page intentionally left blank.

Chapter 4

Movement and Maneuver/Fires and Maneuver (USMC) in Cold Regions

A key task to achieving victory in any operational environment involves successfully emplacing and sustaining forces in time and space to concentrate their combined arms. While easily said, this task is always difficult to achieve. The cold region environment further complicates this task by presenting challenges not found in milder climates. The *movement and maneuver warfighting function* is the related tasks and systems that move forces to achieve a position of advantage in relation to the enemy. Direct fire is inherent in maneuver, as is close combat (FM 3-0). The *fires warfighting function* is the related tasks and systems that provide collective and coordinated Army indirect fires, joint fires, and command and control warfare, including nonlethal fires, through the targeting process (FM 3-0). For the Marine Corps, the fires warfighting function refers to those means used to delay, disrupt, degrade, or destroy enemy capabilities, forces, or facilities as well as affect the enemy's will to fight. The maneuver warfighting function is the movement of forces for the purpose of gaining an advantage over the enemy (MCRP 5-12C). This chapter discusses movement by individuals, by vehicles, over water, and by air.

MOVEMENT BY INDIVIDUALS

4-1.   Individual snow movement techniques prove the most reliable form of transportation in the cold region environment. Ideally, Soldiers and Marines who deploy to a cold region environment should be familiar with and trained in equipment that facilitates individual movement.

EQUIPMENT

4-2.   There are three major individual movement techniques: snowshoeing, skiing, and skijoring. Each technique has its own unique planning considerations, advantages, and disadvantages. In general, personnel will not need special equipment in snow less than 12 inches (30 centimeters) deep. When the snow cover is deeper than 12 inches (30 centimeters), leaders consider special cold region movement techniques that use skis and snowshoes. The Army has recently started to field special kits to aid in movement. These kits aid in movement and maneuver in both cold and mountainous regions. Units that need these kits should contact the Army Mountain Warfare School, Northern Warfare Training Center, or Marine Corps Mountain Warfare Training Center for further information since these kits continually evolve.

Snowshoes

4-3.   At a minimum, all Soldiers and Marines should possess the ability to use snowshoes. Snowshoes are the easiest to use and most easily trained method for movement in the cold region environment. When Soldiers and Marines are in rough terrain, find themselves in thick brush, or lack the equipment or time to become proficient with skis, they should use snowshoes. Units can easily implement a unit training plan for snowshoes.

Skis

4-4.   Skis enable Soldiers and Marines to move quickly into remote areas that vehicles cannot access since they allow for much quicker infiltration and exfiltration than snowshoes. Skis work particularly well for missions such as raids and reconnaissance and surveillance. However, most individuals will not require skis. Specialized units such as Rangers, Special Forces, and Scouts will have utility for skis. The disadvantage to skis is that they take a long time to train on and require the purchase of special equipment. The Northern Warfare Training Center provides a standard estimate that it will take 40 to 50 hours for most Soldiers to attain proficiency using skis with the standard combat load. Skiing expertise is only maintained in a few Army schools. If commanders deem this as a crucial skill, they should contact the Northern Warfare Training Center, the Army's Mountain Warfare School, 10th Special Forces, or Marine Corps Mountain Warfare Training Center to receive training for this task.

Skijoring

4-5.   Skijoring is a method of pulling individuals on skis with a snowmobile or small unit support vehicle (SUSV) (see paragraph 4-44 for more information on the latter). It takes very little energy to hold onto the rope and be pulled along. Skijoring effectively moves personnel and equipment to a staging area quickly. Although it depends on the model of the SUSV, all equipment normally carried by Soldiers and Marines will be placed in the vehicle. Soldiers and Marines will only have their uniform and assigned weapon on their person while skijoring. Like skiing, skijoring is training intensive. Personnel must also ensure that they cover all exposed skin since they will be traveling up to 15 miles (24 kilometers) per hour while skijoring.

4-6.   When Soldiers and Marines perfect movement techniques, leaders execute careful route planning for cold region movement. Key considerations include:

- Conduct a map reconnaissance. Going around terrain features may be faster than going over these terrain features. Leaders check the contour and select the flattest route with the least amount of ascending and descending.
- Decide if personnel will use skis or snowshoes. Check the proficiency of individuals. Determine which route (and its terrain) individuals can best negotiate.
- Decide if personnel will carry heavy rucksacks or pull sleds. Check the predicted temperatures during movement.
- Determine if and how Soldiers and Marines will camouflage their tracks. In barren areas, or areas above the tree line, tracks may be difficult if not impossible to conceal. In open terrain, personnel want to break only one set of tracks. Aircraft flying over can more easily spot several tracks than a single set of tracks.
- Decide if the route is feasible during conditions of limited visibility that often occur in cold region environments.
- Check if the route crosses any potential avalanche areas. As far as avalanche prone slopes are concerned, avoid them at all costs.
- Identify potential obstacles. Check if streams and other bodies of water have frozen sufficiently to support troops and vehicles. Check the water level in streams. Determine if individuals can negotiate high snow banks. Check if plowed roads perpendicular to the route have high banks of plowed snow.

4-7.   The normal planning rate for troops on hard-packed, gently rolling terrain is 2.5 miles (4 kilometers) per hour. When crossing snow or hilly terrain, this rate decreases. Table 4-1 (page 4-3) helps leaders judge the approximate rate of march for troops. These figures were calculated with personnel wearing the typical combat load. Terrain angle (elevation) also affects mobility. If a unit moves uphill, add one hour for every 1,000 feet (304 meters) increase in elevation. While it may seem counterintuitive, experience has shown that troops traveling downhill often experience problems. Therefore, leaders should plan one hour of extra travel time for every 1,600 feet (488 meters) of decrease in elevation.

4-8.   The terms broken and unbroken trail have specific meanings. When moving through undisturbed—or unbroken—snow greater than 12 inches (30 centimeters), the lead two or three personnel have to pack the snow for the rest of the file. Once accomplished, the trail then becomes broken. The lead personnel will exert more effort and will need to be cycled to the rear of the formation every 15 to 30 minutes. Personnel complete this cycling in much the same way they execute a last man up run. Leaders replace personnel in the lead every 15 to 30 minutes depending on fitness level. If dismounted, troops deploy into column (wedge) formation outside the file formation, and then the unit will move more slowly. With no one breaking the trail, all personnel must now move through undisturbed snow. In temperate regions, column formation is ideal since it maximizes fields of fire and allows for greater command and control. However, when operating in a cold region environment, the ideal formation is the file formation. Leaders only deploy into column formation if enemy contact is imminent because the rate of movement is so constrained.

Table 4-1. Rates of march for individual movement

Movement Mode	Unbroken Trail	Broken Trail
On foot, no ski or snowshoe Less than 1 foot (30 centimeters) of snow	1.5 to 3 kph	2 to 3 kph
On foot, no ski or snowshoe More than 1 foot (30 centimeters) of snow	.5 to 1 kph	2 to 3 kph
Snowshoe	1.5 to 3 kph	3 to 4 kph
Skiing	1.5 to 5 kph	5 to 6 kph
Skijoring	not applicable	8 to 24 kph (for safety, 15 kph is the highest recommended speed)
kph kilometers per hour		
time/distance formula: Add 1 hour for every 300 meters of ascent and 1 hour for every 600 meters of decent.		

4-9. Tracks from tanks and infantry fighting vehicles provide trails for dismounted infantry. Such broken trails add speed to the operation and provide ease of movement. In addition, Soldiers and Marines will not need to concern themselves about laid mines.

Kits and Sleds

4-10. The Army and Marine Corps have recently started to field special kits to aid in movement. These kits aid in movement and maneuver in both cold and mountainous regions. Units that need these kits should contact the Army Mountain Warfare School, the Northern Warfare Training Center, or the Marine Corps Mountain Warfare Training Center for information on the latest version of these kits. These kits continually evolve so this manual will not discuss individual ones.

4-11. Many units may find that using smaller sleds are desirable. For example, the Marines employ a four man sled design. There are many designs available for commercial off-the-shelf purchase. These sleds are well suited for squad movements and surveillance and reconnaissance missions.

METHODS TO USE EQUIPMENT

4-12. To obtain the maximum advantage of snowshoes and skis, Soldiers and Marines should use snowshoes and skis as long as far forward as possible and drop them at the assault position, leaving them behind only when they can reach the objective more quickly and easily on foot. The small-unit leader decides at which phase in the attack troops should travel on foot. Generally, personnel leave skis at the assault position. Soldiers and Marines can execute close combat on foot more effectively and more easily than if on skis.

4-13. Conversely, deep snow may force units to close into the objective on skis. Individuals using snowshoes may keep them on through all phases of the attack. Under favorable snow conditions, they may pile skis together at the assault position. Leaders may also direct individuals to fasten this equipment on their bodies in a position where the equipment will least hinder them.

4-14. As friendly forces approach the effective range of enemy weapons, they move by fire and maneuver. The individuals proceed by short rushes on foot, skis, or snowshoes—whichever is most feasible. Rushing on foot, individuals drag skis with one hand and the weapon in the other hand. Individuals can hold the skis and poles in one hand by holding the skis together at the tips with the poles through the two straps. Troops can also tie the skis to their belt and drag them.

4-15. When the unit does not expect contact with the enemy, Soldiers and Marines carry their weapons across their backs. Each weapon is slung over either shoulder, the butt at the individual's side or attached to the rucksack (if carried by the individual). When contact with the enemy is imminent, Soldiers and Marines sling the weapons around their necks and in front of their bodies thus releasing both arms for rapid skiing. When contact with the enemy has been established, the individual carries the weapon in one hand and the ski poles in the other so the weapon is ready for action. When firing from a standing position with skis, troops can use the ski poles by holding them in the supporting hand and resting the weapon at the intersection of the two poles. See figure 4-1.

Figure 4-1. Standing firing position with skis

4-16. Under conditions where the depth of the snow is less than 50 centimeters (20 inches), Soldiers and Marines can leave skis behind when in the attack position. They take this action if it becomes evident that they can launch an attack on foot more rapidly and efficiently than on skis.

4-17. As soon as the unit seizes the objective, troops recover and bring forward their skis, ski poles, or snowshoes. A two-man team can quickly make a ski bundle and drag the skis of the entire squad at one time.

4-18. In deep, loose snow under hostile fire, it may be more advantageous to advance in a high-crawl position. Soldiers and Marines move with their skis by holding the skis through the toe straps and taking full advantage of snowdrifts and bushes. They can use snowshoes in the same manner.

4-19. Sliding forward in a low crawl on skis is another method of advancing, especially over firm snow. Soldiers and Marines can sling the rifle over the shoulder or lay it on the skis directly in front of them. The latter is possible only when the snow is hard so that it cannot get into the rifle.

4-20. In deep snow, personnel can dig trenches in the snow leading in the direction of the objective when it is too difficult to be reached by over snow movement. They dig snow trenches on a zigzag course by throwing the snow out under cover of darkness or, in an emergency, the digging may be masked by smokescreens. They place the snow shoveled from the trench on the enemy side of the trench to protect crawling individuals from enemy observation.

MOVEMENT BY VEHICLES

4-21. Much like individual movement in a cold region environment, vehicle movement in cold region environment requires following certain fundamentals. Soldiers and Marines must consider terrain and environmental factors when operating vehicles in the cold. Driving conditions are more favorable in winter when terrain is frozen and units can use vehicles more easily. Areas such as bogs, muskeg, rivers, and lakes that units could not pass in spring, summer, and fall now afford the opportunity for leaders to bring mounted forces to bear.

4-22. Soldiers and Marines must pay careful attention to the details before moving or maneuvering across frozen or snow-covered terrain. They consider the weight of the vehicle and payload, terrain, weather (will the road thaws in the near future due to increased temperatures), and ice thickness and composition. If they fail to account for these details, then units will suffer loss of equipment and personnel.

ROUTE SELECTION

4-23. Soldiers and Marines will find that routes in cold region environment are limited. Terrain, season, distance from established facilities, and lack of road networks constrain ground forces in this type of environment from both an administrative movement and maneuver standpoint. To select the best routes possible for the movement and maneuver of forces, leaders consider maps, engineer support, reconnaissance, quality of roads, and waterways.

4-24. Map data for cold region environments may be inaccurate or outdated. Leaders should conduct a detailed reconnaissance of the area to verify the information. While this may take extra time, it will save lives, resources, and combat power further into the operation. Effective leaders rely on brigade terrain teams and use tools such as special geographic information system software to execute terrain analysis and mobility studies.

4-25. Routes through cold region environments require extensive engineer support to construct, expand, and maintain. If units need to construct new routes, engineers should select the routes that take advantage of natural cover, gain concealment from air observation, and avoid steep slopes, abrupt ravines, unfrozen swamps, open streams, and other obstacles. In winter, low terrain usually provides the best routes.

4-26. If a potential axis of advance needs to go through forested areas, then units conduct a detailed reconnaissance for lanes they may need to widen. Edges of forest often prove the most suitable for this option. Leaders select routes in forests where trees are widely spaced and, if possible, in sandy soil. This will make it easier for heavy equipment to break trail and clear trees.

4-27. Units often use tanks or bulldozers to break trails; in some cases, they even use armored personnel carriers. As soon as possible, bulldozers improve the route by pushing off broken timber and, in winter, the excess snow. Units improve the road to carry all the tracked equipment and to be at least one-lane wide with sufficient turnouts for returning traffic. At times, trail breaking vehicles may have to deviate slightly from the route selected by the reconnaissance unit to avoid open water and excessive slopes. However, the main supply route (MSR) able to carry all tracked vehicles of the unit normally follows the selected route.

4-28. Military movement can use waterways if they have equipment or improvised rafts. With detailed current reconnaissance, tracked vehicles can use streams, creeks, and graveled riverbeds as routes through muskeg areas. However, troops must conduct a detailed reconnaissance and mobility study before pursuing this course of action.

TRAVERSING TERRAIN DURING FREEZE AND THAW CYCLES

4-29. Soldiers and Marines may find themselves traversing terrain during freeze and thaw cycles that occur in spring and fall. Generally, frozen ground can increase vehicle mobility, while thawing ground nearly always reduces mobility. While these generalities are true, movement can still occur during these times.

Types of Freezing and Thawing Terrain

4-30. Vehicle operation on freezing ground is characterized by the ability of the ground to fully support the vehicle. For unfrozen soils that are not extremely difficult to traverse, the presence of 5 centimeters of frost at the surface usually allows unlimited cross-country operations. Normally untrafficable terrain may require a substantial frost layer before vehicle operations are possible. Certain "soft" terrain stands to gain considerable strength upon freezing. For example, the compressive strength of frozen peat can be 350 to 400 times its unfrozen strength, making it possible to operate vehicles in peat areas when they are frozen.

4-31. Three critical conditions exist for vehicle mobility on freezing and thawing soils illustrated in figure 4-2.

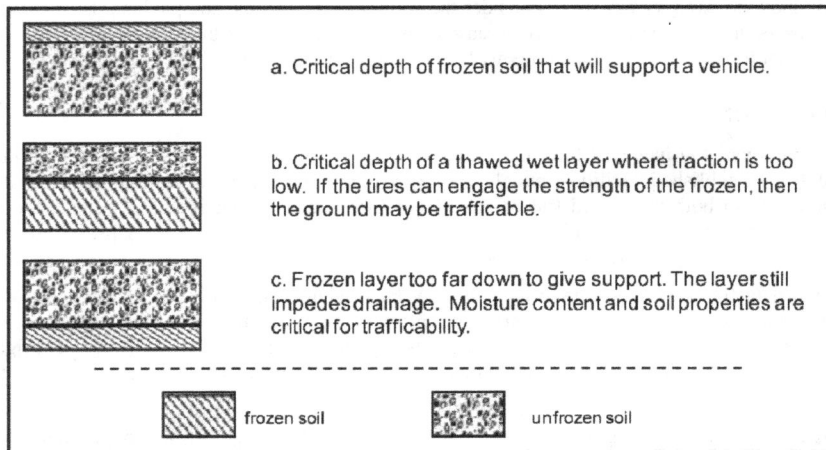

Figure 4-2. Critical conditions for trafficability of freezing or thawing ground

4-32. When a wet, weak soil begins to freeze (see figure 4-2a), the strong frozen layer on top increases the bearing capacity of the ground. The bearing capacity—the ability of the soil to support a vehicle—is determined by the frost depth and the relative wetness of the frozen ground surface. During spring and intermittent thaws, a thawed layer of soil develops over the frozen soil (see figure 4-2b). In the top layer, the soil moisture is higher than normal due to snowmelt. The shallow thawed layer traps this moisture creating a wet and weak layer of soil over the stronger frozen layer. Reduced vehicle mobility is determined by the bearing strength and "slipperiness" (low traction) of the composite soil, expressed as thaw depth and the soil moisture in the thawed layer. As the thaw progresses deeper (see figure 4-2c), the frozen layer becomes too distant to add support to the vehicle or strength to the effective soil system, but it often continues to restrict the soil drainage adding to wet, low-traction conditions. The mobility modeling for freezing ground is limited to go/no-go predictions based on whether the ground can support the vehicle.

4-33. Little data exists for vehicle traction on frozen ground. In general, frozen ground enhances mobility and traction. However, if the ground has a high ice content or if the temperature is near melting, then the traction and mobility decrease. In these cases, traction may be reduced because of the slipperiness of the surface and may be closer to the level of traction experienced on ice rather than that for the soil alone.

4-34. For vehicle performance, the wet conditions are the most critical. If saturated, the soil can become slippery, reducing traction to 50 percent of normal. In addition, the vehicle will tend to sink down to a soil layer solid enough to support it. Generally, a vehicle moving in thawing or very wet soils can only travel through very wet soils when the depth is less than 2/3 the wheel radius—or up to the vehicle's undercarriage. Table 4-2 lists ground clearances for common military vehicles.

Table 4-2. Ground clearance by military vehicle

Vehicle	Clearance
HMMWV	16 inches (41 centimeters)
M2 Bradley	18 inches (46 centimeters)
M1 Abrams	19 inches (48 centimeters)
Stryker	18 inches (46 centimeters)
LAV25 (Marine Corps Only)	14 inches (36 centimeters)
AMTRAK (Marine Corps Only)	16 inches (41 centimeters)
AMTRAK amphibious tracked vehicle HMMWV high mobility multipurpose wheeled vehicle LAV25 light armored vehicle-25	

4-35. Diurnal effects happen when a surface freezes at night allowing increased trafficability during the morning until thawing occurs during the day. As thaw depth increases, the degradation caused by repeated traffic increases. Units can modify their procedures through untrafficable areas that are caused by thawing soils in low lying, poorly drained areas. Some modifications to standard operating procedures include units—

- Lowering tire pressures (to off-road specifications) to reduce rutting and promote healing of damaged surfaces.
- Traveling at night when ground is frozen.
- Improving the drainage at trouble spots.

Techniques for Stabilizing Thawing Soils

4-36. Often, building a conventional gravel road provides the simplest and most effective means of producing routes for movement of forces. Dump trucks, loaders, and bulldozers are standard equipment. The problem building the roads comes from the availability of material in the cold region environment. Some aggregate sources simply are unavailable. Because thawing can be the cause of the immobility, sources may still be frozen, inaccessible, or of poor quality, and susceptible to thaw weakening.

4-37. Chunk wood is an excellent substitute for gravel. Units create chunk wood by chopping tree pieces in a shredder or chunker. These pieces range in size from 1 to 8 inches (3 to 20 centimeters), depending on the diameter of the tree fed into the shredder. When access roads became impassable, units can use chunk wood to reconstruct and allow passage. Because of its low density, a weak base layer of other material (that might not be capable of supporting heavier aggregate material) can support a layer of chunk wood. Units add gravel above the chunk wood for use as a permanent road. As a base beneath gravel cover, the chunk wood provides an excellent insulating layer to reduce detrimental effects of frost action in areas of seasonal freezing. Frost action will cause the road surface to deteriorate as the water contracts and expands as it freezes. However, chunk wood's success relies on the availability of a source of trees and the development of a commercial chunker. Engineer assets need to plan in advance to use this technique.

4-38. Tree slash is another inexpensive way to improve roads. Tree slash emplacement requires no special equipment or training, only a source of trees. This method uses branches of trees placed at angles to the direction of travel. Engineers of timber access roads in Alaska often use this method to provide a base for a rock fragment surface. The best method of placing the slash uses the trunks to fill in ruts and hollows. Then individuals lay branches no bigger than 8 centimeters (3 inches) in diameter using a herringbone pattern at 45° angles to the direction of travel. They add more slash during trafficking to replenish the existing surface. Its availability is slightly broader than that of chunk wood simply because personnel can use scrub brush, old cornhusks, or any bulk vegetative material. However, tree slash is labor intensive and could potentially expose construction personnel to enemy fire. It is not a desirable surface for small rubber-tired vehicle passage or foot traffic; walking is extremely difficult. Tree slash can also puncture and damage hydraulic hoses on the underside of equipment.

4-39. Units can use gravel roads, chunk wood, and tree slash in unison if they lack material for a particular construction technique. Units should consult the Cold Regions Research and Engineering Laboratory for more information on this topic.

VEHICLE TYPES

4-40. The Army and Marine Corps use two types of vehicles in the cold region environment: wheeled and tracked. Each phase in the operation must address snow and terrain conditions. Since these conditions change as the operation progresses and weather conditions alter, leaders must understand how the weather impacts wheeled and tracked vehicles.

Wheeled Vehicles

4-41. In general, wheeled vehicles can use only road networks in cold region environments and are of limited utility for movement and maneuver. A depth of 20 inches (0.5 meter) of snow severely delays or immobilizes most wheeled vehicles. Ideally, units will not use wheeled vehicles in more than 12 inches (30 centimeters) of snow. Generally, 2 inches (5 centimeters) or more of frozen soil permits cross-country mobility. Whether a Stryker or high mobility multipurpose wheeled vehicle (HMMWV), all wheeled vehicles share common characteristics that restrict their use in the cold region environment. Even in the dead of winter when the ground is frozen, wheeled vehicle movement has problems. Terrain is uneven and some features will not entirely freeze. When drivers cross this terrain, they often experience slippery spots and slide off the road, immobilizing the vehicle. To complicate the situation more, drivers often need recovery assets and sometimes even these cannot reach the immobilized vehicle. Recovery assets also run the risk of becoming immobilized themselves. Units need additional combat forces to provide security for a recovery operation.

Tracked Vehicles

4-42. The Army uses light and heavy tracked vehicles in the cold region environment. Regardless of their weight, all tracked vehicles consider the saturation of the snow. Wet snow from a depth of 24 to 29 inches (60 to 75 centimeters) slows most tracked vehicles. Wet clinging snow also tends to accumulate on the tracks, suspension idler wheels, and sprockets. Units often stop to remove wet snow. Dry snow causes few operating difficulties as it has little tendency to pack on suspensions systems.

4-43. The permafrost layer under tundra is between 6 to 24 inches (15 to 61 centimeters) deep. That depth enables tracked vehicles to gain some traction. Leaders still must exercise caution. Units take measurements of the permafrost layer to ensure tracked vehicles do not sink into the tundra or muskeg. While tracked vehicles can operate somewhat effectively, it is impossible to employ wheeled assets in this terrain. Leaders should keep this in mind when considering resupply and maintenance needs in tundra or muskeg.

Light Tracked Vehicles

4-44. The Army's most mobile tracked platform for operating in cold region environments is the SUSV. Despite its advanced ability to move over ice and snow, units use the SUSV only in support of maneuver elements due to its lack of armor. There is an armored version (M973 A2) capable of stopping small arms, but these are limited in number. The SUSV can move 180 miles (290 kilometers) on a full tank of fuel traveling 6 to 12 miles (10 to 20 kilometers) per hour cross-country and up to 19 miles (30 kilometers) per hour on flat areas. It can carry up to 13 personnel depending on the configuration of the front compartment and can skijor up to 30 personnel depending on the length of rope. The SUSV's ability to carry so many troops such a far distance enables it to emplace dismounted troops quickly. A CH-47 helicopter can sling load the SUSV and deliver it to remote destinations with light forces. Refer to table 4-2 for Marine Corps vehicles.

4-45. The design of the SUSV distinctively differs from other tracked vehicles. Overall, its weight is light and its tracks are wide. Its special tracks float over the snow instead of using the vehicle's weight to sink to the ground to gain traction. The SUSV complements light forces because it can tow lighter pieces of artillery. This is a crucial combat multiplier for light infantry engaged in combat operations.

Heavy Tracked Vehicles

4-46. Heavy tracked vehicles can include main battle tanks and M88s. They negotiate dry snow of 3 to 6 feet (1 to 2 meters) in depth. However, units often consider 5 feet (1.5 meters) the point at which track vehicles will experience delays or even immobilization. Users should exercise caution before employing tracked vehicles in deep snow. Tracked vehicles can maintain normal speeds after several heavy vehicles form a passage creating a packed snow trail. The surface of a packed snow trail compacts into a hard mass resembling well-packed wet sand and is easily traversed by all types of vehicles.

4-47. Soldiers and Marines may need to modify their tracks with machine tools to operate effectively in the cold region environment. Rubber does not gain traction on ice effectively. Conversely, rubber is good for gaining traction if the vehicle sinks into the muskeg or tundra. Units should plan to have additional tracks on hand because the rubber has half the lifecycle that it does in more temperate regions. Specific vehicles have special considerations:

- The M2 Bradley does not have a special track cleat for traction during winter. Drivers can remove the track shoe pads for better traction in muddy, snowy, or icy conditions.
- The M88-series family of vehicles also does not have a special track cleat for snow and ice. The only time to reverse the center guides is during icy conditions. Even then, personnel only reverse the center guide on every fourth shoe and only after modifying the center guide. Essentially, this cuts it down a few inches so it will grip, not impale.
- The Army has authorized that personnel can remove track pads on the M1 Abrams to improve traction. However, this method can damage track components while providing only limited traction. For tanks with T158/T158LL tracks, the Army has special ice cleats available to prevent all that slipping and sliding. No traction aids are available for the T156 track.

VEHICULAR CONSIDERATIONS

4-48. Most military materiel is designed to operate without modification at ambient (the surrounding air) temperatures to -25 °F (-32 °C) and with modification to -50 °F (-46 °C). At these temperatures, personnel prepare for changes in materiel. They maintain all equipment in the best mechanical condition to withstand the added difficulties of operating properly during sub-zero operations. See FM 9-207 and applicable technical manuals for a more detailed listing of technical issues that vehicles experience in cold regions.

Antifreeze, Fuels, Hydraulic Fluids, Lubricants

4-49. Operating in the cold region environment requires more petroleum, oils, lubricants, and fuel. Vehicles operating in the cold region environment have increased idling, increased heating needs, and difficulty in movement resulting in less efficient operation. Lubricants, fuels, and hydraulic fluids increase in viscosity as temperatures decrease. Unless properly specified for operations in extreme cold temperatures, they can gel or harden, damaging or making equipment inoperable. According to FM 9-207, antifreeze, hydraulic fluids, and lubricants must be specified for cold operations at temperatures to -65 °F (-54 °C). Even specified fluids developed for cold operations can still differ in the viscosity as temperatures get colder. For example at these temperatures, JP-8, which is the single fuel used in military diesel engines, should atomize for the correct fuel-air mixtures, but there may still be difficulty with combustion and gelling.

4-50. Wind chill has an adverse effect on vehicles just as it does on people. Personnel must maintain sufficiently high temperatures for normal operation of both the engine and other components. While wind speed has no affect on the actual measured air temperature, it strongly affects the rate of heat loss. Heat loss always increases with wind speed, but the proportional increase is most significant at low wind speeds. That is, an increase in wind speed from 0 to 16 feet (5 meters) per second results in far greater increase in heat loss than that from 32 to 49 feet (10 to 15 meters) per second.

4-51. Wind chill has several important implications. First, when the engine is shut down, it will cool to ambient temperature much faster in windy conditions, and drivers will need to use cold-starting procedures to restart it. Second, parts of the machine that are more exposed to environmental conditions, such as the drive elements or transmission, may warm very little, if at all, and will cool down faster at shutdown. Third, components that require heating to operate smoothly (such as payload mechanisms) require greater heating power to maintain the necessary operating temperatures.

4-52. High heat loss can create problems similar to those created by starting up equipment too abruptly after it has been cold soaked. Even if the engine itself has warmed sufficiently for normal operation, remote parts of the machine that are still quite cold can be damaged by placing too great a load on them too soon. Stiffened lubricants, including hydraulic fluids, can place abnormally high loads on joints and linkages. Seals can break. Structural elements can bend or crack. Drive train elements can snap. Drivers must initiate operation slowly in very cold temperatures and continue slower-than-normal operation if the initial stiffness does not fully abate.

Batteries

4-53. Because chemical reactions proceed more slowly as the temperature decreases, a cold soaked battery's available energy sharply decreases. Depending on the power draw, the battery may be inadequate to power or start equipment. In addition, cold batteries have a slower rate of recharging because of the slowed chemical reactions. Discharged batteries are more subject to damage because of freezing. Personnel must thaw a frozen battery completely before attempting to recharge it.

4-54. Lead-acid batteries become vulnerable to freezing when discharged, do not charge well when cold, and lose power at low temperatures. However, they are inexpensive and have been used extensively in automotive and construction equipment in cold region environments. A good practice is to warm up lead-acid batteries before cold starting the engine or charging the batteries.

4-55. Nickel-cadmium (NiCd) batteries perform better than lead-acid batteries at low temperatures. They are unlikely to freeze and have better cranking power and charge acceptance for the same temperature. They are, however, more expensive.

4-56. Nickel-metal hydride (NiMH) batteries have higher energy density than NiCd batteries. However, they lose more capacity at low temperatures than NiCd and lead-acid batteries, and below 32 °F (0 °C), charging is not advisable. Personnel must charge both NiCd and NiMH batteries at reduced rates below 59 °F (15 °C).

4-57. Lithium-ion batteries experience relatively little capacity loss at low temperatures and can be charged at normal rates above 32 °F (0 °C). Charging at reduced rates can occur as low as -22 °F (-30 °C). Although Lithium-ion batteries are more expensive than NiCd and NiMH, they can be the battery of choice for hybrid-electric drive systems where their higher energy density offsets their higher cost. Superior cold-weather performance is then an added benefit.

Other Common Cold Region Vehicular Problems

4-58. Rubber and synthetic rubber gradually stiffen as they cool although they may retain most of their elasticity until about -20 °F (-29 °C). Rubber will continue to remain somewhat flexible until approximately -60 °F (-51 °C), when it becomes brittle. It will also become brittle if it remains at -0 °F (-29 °C) over a long period. Under these conditions, Soldiers and Marines must handle cables and hoses with care. The polymer covering on cables may break from shock loads and bending. It can be almost impossible to re-coil cables or rubber hoses once they are cold soaked without re-warming them. Hoses may crack, increasing the potential for fuel, oil, and other fluid spills.

4-59. Fabrics, like canvas covers used on military vehicles, can become extremely difficult to fold or smooth out in cold temperatures and in some cases must be warmed first. Plastics and other polymers become brittle in cold weather and may break because of cold and vibration.

4-60. Manufacturers provide winterization kits for military equipment. For anticipated temperatures of -25 °F (-32 °C) or lower, units install personnel heater kits and hardtop closures on military vehicles. Leaders should not attempt operations in areas where temperatures often fall from -25 °F (-32 °C) to -65 °F (-54 °C) without winterization kits. Since some winterization kits require use at temperatures warmer than -25 °F (-32 °C), consult the technical manual for that individual piece of equipment.

4-61. The cold may adversely affect all subsystems of a vehicle—engine starting and operation, brake system, suspension, tracks or tires—before, during, and after operations. Personnel must pay appropriate attention to these subsystems.

4-62. Military vehicles are required to start without an additional heat source down to -25 °F (-32 °C). Below this temperature, drivers can use a heat source to warm the engine. For gasoline engines, a successful start in cold weather requires that the viscosity of the engine lubricating oil permits cranking and that the battery be fully charged and warm enough to supply adequate cranking current and ignition spark. Diesel engines are particularly difficult to start in cold weather without preheating the intake air or using other means of raising combustion temperature. Since the engine heats the air by compression, it must attain a temperature hot enough to ignite the injected fuel. Follow the operator's manual for starting and operation in the cold.

4-63. Drivers can preheat engines following certain procedures:

- Ensure all preheating systems, such as glow plugs or fuel fired preheaters, are operating properly prior to use.
- Use air manifold heaters when the engine is turned over. Switch off the air manifold heater when the engine starts.
- If so equipped, operate the engine coolant fuel-fired preheater for the prescribed amount of time before starting.
- Use glow plugs to pre-heat the air in the cylinder prior to starting the engine.
- Inject chemicals, such as ether, which more easily ignites at low temperatures.
- Raise the compression ratio to increase the charge temperature.

4-64. Hydraulic brakes generally use a brake fluid that is capable of all season use. Cold temperatures seriously affect air brakes. Moisture released from compressed air may freeze in the tank, lines, or valves. This frozen moisture in the brake system may prevent proper brake operation. Brake lines, air brake filters, brake chambers, pushrods, valves, and seals are prone to more defects and failure in cold. Condensation that accumulates between brake shoes and brake drums while the vehicles is moving may freeze when the vehicle stops, making it difficult for the vehicle to move. Army vehicles, including the family of medium tactical vehicles, heavy equipment transporter, palletized load system, and HMMWV heavy variant, have central tire inflation systems that operate off an air compressor. Frozen air valves and air leaks often cause locked brakes or flat tires.

4-65. Shock absorbers may not operate correctly in cold weather because of increased viscosity of the fluid, seals in the shock absorber leaking, and metal becoming brittle. Problems with shock absorbers result in a vehicle that usually has a harsher ride, increased stress on other suspension parts, and broken shock absorbers. To prevent damage to the shock absorber, the operating rod, or the mounting brackets during extreme cold, drivers may need to operate the vehicle slowly for the first few miles until the oil in the shock absorbers warms.

4-66. Tires become rigid in the cold, and at temperatures below about -40 °F (-40 °C) after being parked in one spot, the tires may develop flat spots where the tire touches the ground. The tires will round out when the vehicle moves and the tires warm, but this will also cause additional vibration. Extreme cold temperatures can cause sidewalls to become brittle and to crack. Personnel inflate tires to the proper pressure. Since tire pressure changes with temperature, they must adjust a tire inflated to the correct pressure indoors to the lower pressure at a cold temperature. Generally, personnel check tire inflation in the cold and adjust it appropriately. Central tire inflation systems may fail to operate properly and maintain adequate pressure.

4-67. Cold temperatures cause problems in springs, hydraulic systems, and air filters. Springs become brittle and break easily at low temperatures. Personnel correctly and securely mount and maintain mechanical fasteners, moving parts, and systems subjected to high stresses. Hydraulic systems may have a slow response because of the increased fluid viscosity. This can affect power steering systems, automatic transmissions, and other hydraulically activated systems. Air filters can become plugged from wind-blown or falling snow or from vehicle movement over snow covered roads and trails.

Hours Required for Performing Maintenance on Equipment

4-68. At temperatures below -40 °F (-40 °C), as much as five times the normal maintenance time may be required. Starting and warm-up time is also increased and may approach 2 hours in temperatures of -50 °F (-58 °C). Winter operations require complete winterization, diligent maintenance, and well-trained crews.

4-69. Performance of field maintenance at temperatures below -20 °F (-29 °C) proves extremely difficult unless units provide some type of heated shelter. Maintenance shelter tents, portable shelters, or large tarps and air duct heaters work well when operating in cold region environments.

Recovery Procedures

4-70. When employing motorized transportation in the cold region environment, Soldiers and Marines will inevitably need to execute vehicle recovery operations. Chapter 22 of training circular (TC) 21-305-20 describes procedures for executing these tasks. In addition to this, FM 4-30.31 describes recovery procedures as well as conducting battle damage assessment and recovery. Marines refer to MCRP 4-11.4A for recovery procedures.

MOVEMENT OVER WATER

4-71. Leaders, Soldiers, and Marines operating in cold region environments need to plan for water obstacles and gap crossings. These obstacles are numerous in cold region environments. These obstacles will require bridging assets or rafting assets that only specialized engineer units can provide. Often times, units will not have these assets available and will need to use field expedient methods to employ mounted forces. The field expedient mode used in cold region environments is the ice bridge.

4-72. Units should exercise caution when constructing ice bridges for this type of environment. Both an art and science applies to building ice bridges. In general, rivers with slow currents, lakes, and deep swamps will freeze to a point that allows ice crossings in winter and well into spring. However, leaders must pay special attention to shorelines, weather, and river conditions. Ice is thinner near the shore so units may need to build ramps. If the temperature rises above freezing shortly after completing the ice bridge, then units will have wasted a lot of time and effort. Leaders consider the type of river. Glacial fed rivers are unpredictable. They have swift currents, they surge and recede quickly, and the course of the river changes frequently.

4-73. Construction of an ice bridge requires pumps or some other means of flooding the ice and freezing temperatures. Temperatures below 10 °F (50 °C) work best. If the ice is exposed to direct sunlight or the temperature is above 25 °F (77 °C), units flood the area in the evening to take advantage of the colder night temperatures. The time units spend selecting a good site results in reduced construction and maintenance effort. It takes less effort to conduct an adequate reconnaissance of a crossing site than to extract a vehicle that has broken through the ice. An ideal site, within the tactical limitations, provides the best combination of shortest distance, gradual sloping embankments, and low turbulence. The natural ice should be at least 10 centimeters (4 inches) thick to support men and equipment required to construct the ice bridge. Personnel ensure that water is flowing under the ice and that no hot springs are present. Hot springs would make building an ice bridge impossible. For details of ice bridge construction, refer to FM 3-90.12/ MCWP 3-17.1 and FM 3-34.343.

4-74. Leaders, Soldiers, and Marines can also consider fording. In general, units can ford shallow rivers with stable beds. Before fording, units remove large obstructions and verify that the current runs less than 1.5 miles per hour. Consult technical manuals for specific instructions and requirements for each vehicle. FM 3-90.12/MCWP 3-17.1 also contains special instructions for fording.

MOVEMENT BY AIR

4-75. Commanders can and must integrate Army aviation effectively into offensive operations. They consider airmobile operations normal rather than special in cold regions. Vertical envelopment, diversionary attacks, and rapid displacement of supporting weapons and reserves fall within the offensive capabilities of an airmobile force. Low troop density throughout the battle area plus flexibility in route selection reduces the hazards of enemy operations and counteraction against movement.

4-76. Aviation is the preferred mode of travel in the cold region environment despite its limitations. Because tracked and wheeled vehicles have so many limitations, aviation takes on a greater importance in cold region environments. Most aviation assets used in the cold region environment will be rotary-wing aircraft.

CHALLENGES

4-77. While preferred for travel in the cold region environment, aviation assets have many unique challenges to overcome.

Temperature

4-78. In general, aviators assume a large degree of risk conducting operations in -40 °F (-40 °C) or lower. The metals in the airframe become brittle and the engines face mechanical difficulty during start up and operation. Many of the electronic instruments that aviators use to assist them during flight become nonoperational or face severe problems at temperatures of -20 °F (-29 °C) or below.

4-79. Pilots keep temperatures in the cabin below freezing while transporting troops into a landing zone (LZ). Temperatures above freezing create condensation on weapons, making them inoperable when troops arrive at the LZ. In addition, personnel keep the doors closed except when Soldiers and Marines are entering or exiting the aircraft.

Visibilty

4-80. Often in cold region environments, the particular weather conditions limit visibility. Aviators require a minimum of 300 feet to fly during day operations and 500 feet during night operations. This problem gets more complicated if carrying a sling-loaded item. If the proper conditions do not exist, then aviators cannot resupply troops, making movement by air somewhat unreliable for planning purposes.

Flying Techniques

4-81. Aviators consider flying techniques during flight operations to maintain security and avoid detection. During flight at less than 40 knots, rotor wash creates a signature identifiable for several miles. Flying at an airspeed above 40 knots displaces the rotor wash horizontally; therefore, little or no blowing snow develops. An airspeed below 40 knots over forested areas can disturb snow in trees, making the flight route easy to detect by the signature left on the trees.

4-82. Aviators do not hover in an aircraft over an external load and attach the sling to the hook in the cold region environment. A 40-foot (12-meter) sling extension allows the pilot to land clear of the load over the weighted end of the sling. Personnel then hook the sling onto the cargo hook. Pilots can take off with less whiteout danger as the aircraft gains 40 to 60 feet (12 to 18 meters) of altitude prior to lifting the heavy external load. Landing an external load with the 40-foot extension is less hazardous as the pilot stays above most of the blowing snow and maintains visual reference while lowering the load to the ground.

Landing Zones

4-83. Planners and leaders also consider suitable LZs for aviation assets. Often units operate in hilly, uneven terrain or thick forests poorly suited to landing aviation assets. Other times, a fine snow covers the LZ, creating whiteout conditions when the aviator attempts to land. Of paramount concern is the risk of flash freeze. Flash freeze occurs when personnel enter the rotor wash area and the kicked-up winds freeze exposed skin. Personnel working in the LZ must cover all skin and minimize their time in this zone. Often, creating a bubble with a 100-foot radius from the aircraft ensures Soldiers and Marines do not fall victim to rotor wash. Soldiers and Marines only enter this bubble when the mission requires and exit as soon possible to avoid injury.

Weight

4-84. The cold region environment adversely affects many of the aircraft's normal flight characteristics. Planners consider these limitations placed on the airframe and plan accordingly. If the aircraft is equipped with ski equipment, it will weigh more and create more drag. The increased air density of cold air helps offset this to a certain degree. The cold also affects the aircraft's payload capability. Crews stow extra fuel containers in the crew compartment. The extra fuel compensates for the extended ranges the aircraft needs to fly and the lack of refueling stations.

PLANNING CONSIDERATIONS

4-85. Typical aviation movement of light forces in a cold region environment requires general planning considerations. Overall, aviation assets effectively overcome the terrain and weather challenges in cold region environments. However, these assets are highly fragile and leaders must not rely solely on aviation for support. Many factors can limit aviation's effectiveness and the amount of combat force it can support.

Types of Aircraft

4-86. The cold region environment uses rotary- and fixed-wing aircraft. The rotary-wing aircraft consist of the CH-47 (known as the Chinook) and the UH-60 (known as the Blackhawk).

4-87. The CH-47 normally transports a maximum of 27 passengers. The operations officer ensures supporting units receive this information. The normal authorized cargo load (ACL) is—
- A total of 27 passengers maximum.
- A total of 27 passengers and 3 ahkios.
- A total of 24 passengers and 4 ahkios.
- For each snowmobile, 2 ahkios or 6 passengers will be deleted from the maximum load.

4-88. The UH-60 normally transports 11 passengers. The operations officer ensures supporting units receive this information. The ACL is—
- A total of 11 passengers maximum.
- A total of 7 passengers and 1 ahkio.

4-89. Units also use fixed-wing aircraft in cold region environments. Many potential landing sites exist in cold region environments. Personnel can construct runways by grading and compacting snow. Airplanes equipped with skis require about 15 percent more landing and takeoff space than those equipped with wheels. Aircraft can use airfields constructed on frozen lakes and rivers after engineers complete a suitable ice reconnaissance.

4-90. On airfields, an ice fog created by fixed-wing aircraft may cover an entire runway. The ice fog can reduce visibility so that other aircraft cannot take off or land if the wind is calm. The ice fog also draws attention to the airfield location.

4-91. Marines reference MCRP 3-35.1A for Marine aviation flight characteristics.

Fire Support

4-92. In general, aviation fire support planning considerations in a cold region do not differ from the planning considerations found in more temperate environments. However, tactical air support takes on more importance since other weapon platforms are limited due to the lack of road networks and terrain. Planners consider and plan for additional assets if available to compensate for the lack of other means of fire support.

4-93. Rarely will aviators use door gunners in cold region operations. With open doors, the gunners, flight crew, and passengers risk getting frostbite too quickly. Attack helicopters provide the suppressive fires. Units may want to eliminate door gunners at other times to increase ground combat power when limited lift is available or distances are greatly extended.

Chapter 5

Sustainment in Cold Regions

Sustainment warfighting function is the related tasks and systems that provide support and services to ensure freedom of action, extend operational reach, and prolong endurance (FM 3-0). The Marine Corps lists logistics instead of sustainment as a warfighting function (see Marine Corps doctrine publication [MCDP] 1-0). The ability to engage and destroy an enemy is only as great as the unit's ability to resupply and sustain itself. This chapter discusses the sustainment plans, their special considerations for the cold region environment, and specific movement requirements.

SUSTAINMENT PLANS

5-1. Development of an adequate sustainment plan requires the commander's close personal attention as well as the participation of the operations and logistics staffs. In a cross-country movement, the operations officer and the logistics officer formulate concepts and prepare detailed plans jointly and concurrently. The operations officer understands, considers, and accepts the limitations of logistic capabilities in a cold region environment. If units plan for operations in cold region environments that exceed the capabilities of sustainment elements, then the overall plan is doomed to failure from the start.

5-2. Sustainment plans become more complex due to the increased severity of the terrain and climate found in cold regions. In more temperate regions, generally a robust and well-developed all-weather transportation network with support facilities helps facilitate military operations. However, in cold region environments, these road networks become scarce and less developed than those found in temperate regions. The same goes for support facilities due to the reduced number of towns. Units address any special equipment needs before deploying and operating in a cold region environment.

CONSIDERATIONS

5-3. Before conducting operations, leaders consider the special equipment needed to conduct their mission and the amount of time it will take to procure this equipment. Typical equipment required for cold region environments includes—

- Skis and ski poles.
- Snowshoes.
- Stoves.
- Sleds such as the ahkio.
- Oversnow vehicles such as the snowmobile.
- Arctic tents.
- Specialized uniforms such as Extended Cold Weather Clothing System (ECWCS) and vapor barrier (known as VB) boots.

5-4. Even if supplies have a national stock number (commonly known as NSN), they may take considerable time to obtain. Generally, the Army stocks limited equipment for a cold region environment in the inventory. Leaders could be forced to consider commercial off-the-shelf equipment.

MOVEMENT REQUIREMENTS

5-5. In predeployment planning, planners evaluate the area of operations for potential lines of communications (LOCs). Key features should include rail networks, usable ports, road networks, and pipelines. Due to the lack of infrastructure in a cold region environment, airfields take on special importance, especially during the early stages of deployment for the units and initial supplies. Depending on the area, ports potentially offer little or no value. Often, ice blocks access to ports, or they are so far removed from the area of operations that their use is impractical.

5-6. Due to the slow rate of resupply and the long distances units cover in the cold region environment, units may need additional support. This support comes from truck companies designated to provide support. These units augment organic assets found in the combat sustainment support battalions or functional transportation units assigned to the sustainment brigade. Additional transportation support may be provided by the logistics civil augmentation program or host-nation support when available. The length of the LOC and the tonnage to move dictates the number of augmentation units needed.

5-7. With adequate reconnaissance and engineer support, frozen rivers may prove better routes for movement. Units must exercise caution since surface ice thickness varies according to local conditions.

5-8. When possible, units use certain vehicles. The heavy expanded mobility tactical truck (known as a HEMTT) and M1074 and M1075 palletized load systems work best on the terrain found in cold region environments. These vehicles have increased mobility due to their design. To facilitate the distribution of supplies, these vehicles can haul prepackaged containers express (CONEXs) and drop them with no materials handling equipment.

5-9. Units strictly control movement to prevent congestion and delay on limited road networks. Due to the extended LOCs in which convoys operate, units incorporate a robust air defense plan since the enemy will rely upon air power to disrupt resupply.

5-10. Field manual-interim (FMI) 4-93.2 discusses sustainment requirements. This manual provides planning guidance for staff and unit officers and a digest of operational data for operators and users who interact with the sustainment brigade. Marines refer to MCWP 4-11 for sustainment.

SUPPLY

5-11. Units stack all supplies stored in the open on pallets or dunnage to keep them from freezing to the ground. Troops locate stacks in areas to minimize the effects of drifting snow. Snow fences can help offset blowing snow. Units mark supplies subject to drifting snow with poles and small flags since a snowstorm may bury these items in the snow. Troops accurately survey large storage facilities from permanent landmarks so that snowplow blades do not damage materials buried in the snow.

5-12. The cold affects the different classes of supply in unique ways that planners consider. This manual describes how units can compensate for the effects of the cold on each class of supply. FMI 4-93.2 describes the general level of supplies that modular forces keep on hand. Marines refer to MCWP 4-11.

Class I

5-13. Units may use intermodal CONEXs to store rations requiring protection from weather but not requiring heated storage. Units store nonperishable rations without heat but pay close attention to the temperature to avoid damaging by freezing and thawing. Prepared meals are preferred but not always practical for feeding. If prepared meals are unavailable, Soldiers and Marines will still need to eat in a warm shelter.

5-14. Units carry a three-day supply of meals in the event resupply efforts falter. Units issue squad and individual stoves with rations so Soldiers and Marines can thaw rations even in the severe cold. Operations on a sustained basis require greater amounts of food because of the increased physical demands on the body. Personnel can also use these stoves to generate water by melting snow and ice. Soldiers and Marines must bring water to a rolling boil for sanitation. These stoves have the added benefit of reducing the weight troops carry.

Water

5-15. Soldiers should use the following information in conjunction with FM 10-52. Marines refer to MCWP 4-11.6. Operators of the reverse osmosis water purification unit (ROWPU) find it difficult to find water in the cold region environment. The extreme temperatures diminish water production and cause stored water to freeze. The optimal temperature for water purification is 77 °F (25 °C). ROWPU operators have three methods to keep water temperature as close to the optimal as possible.

5-16. First, they erect tents over storage bags. This reduces heat loss to the air and neutralizes the wind chill factor. By throwing hay on the ground, operators insulate bags from losing heat to the ground. When they distribute the water through hoses, they will encounter additional problems. They can circulate heated water through distribution hoses, but severe cold makes this difficult to maintain.

5-17. Second, they take a M1077 flatrack, enclose it with plywood and insulation to minimize heat loss, and place two 500-gallon collapsible water tanks in it. Units chain the tanks to the floor with a distribution pump and a commercial heater. Units can easily load and haul the tanks to the field for distribution and then reload it and take it to the nearest potable water source for resupply.

5-18. Troops establish bath and laundry units as soon as possible to reduce the risk of cold injuries and enhance morale. Units construct these sites as close to the water source as possible to minimize the chance of water freezing between the source and the user. To avoid the problem of ice buildup created by the discharge of bath and laundry units, units must move discharge piping as far from the bath site as possible.

5-19. The problem of supplying water in cold regions to units up to battalion size or modular brigades is much greater than that of individual supply. For instance, melting snow and ice on stoves, burners, or open fires in sufficient quantities to provide water for all the needs of large units is impractical because a large amount of fuel is needed to obtain a small amount of water. Seventeen cubic inches of loose snow, when melted, yields only 1 cubic inch of water. Melting snow is not recommended for supplying water in quantity except in an emergency. The chief sources of water supply for large units in the order of their efficiency and economy are drawing water from under river or lake ice, melting ice, melting snow, and well drilling (semipermanent and permanent camps).

5-20. When possible, units locate water points on lakes and rivers on the leeward side where there is generally clearer water, less snowdrifting, and more shelter from the wind. Units position sites on a lake as far from the shore as possible within effective camouflage limitations. To cut holes in ice at water points, ice augers, air tools, steam jets, or other such equipment prove most effective. Units can also drill holes through ice using hand augers. However, shaped charges work far better than hand tools in preparing water holes in thick ice since hand tools cut ice best when ice is less than 24 inches (60 centimeters) thick. Ice usually freezes thinnest where covered by the most snow. The methods used, however, vary with the condition of the ice and with the equipment, personnel, and time available. At low temperatures, troops can keep the hole over the water clear from rapidly forming ice by placing the suction strainer about a foot below the surface when pumping. Continual pumping or insulating the surface keeps the hole clear.

5-21. If large units use snow as a water source, they can shovel it into any available tank or container and heat by any method available. When units use powdered or loosely packed snow for water, they pack it tightly in the container and tamp down or stir it frequently while melting to increase the moisture content and so increase its heat conductivity. Granular snow, usually obtainable near the ground, has higher water content than the lighter snow of the surface layers.

5-22. Because of the normal low turbidity, units can probably provide safe water by chlorination without pretreatment if they accomplish filtration by means of an improved diatomite or ceramic filter. Some treatment problems encountered in cold regions include:

- Water in certain areas requires heavy chlorination to obtain a standard residual test of 0.4 parts per million after a 30-minute contact period in active parts of distribution systems at fixed installations, and of 1 part per million after a 10-minute contact period under field conditions.
- Water softeners and controlled acidity are required in most cases to prevent scaling in heating systems and power plant cooling systems.

5-23. Units in the field can store water in insulated 5-gallon (19-liter) cans. They often use immersion-type heaters to prevent freezing of a water supply tank or trailer.

5-24. Units handle field distribution of water to men and small units in several ways. For immediate use, men or units may fill their containers directly from the source. If they do this, they sterilize the water by boiling it for at least 5 minutes or treating it with individual water purification tablets if not already sterilized. As units pump the water from beneath the ice, they fill unit mobile storage tanks with water and then dispense it to troops. Individuals may furnish their own cooking and drinking water by melting snow or ice. All field water distribution units have insulation or some form of heating device to keep the water in liquid state.

5-25. Transportation of water by truck works well only when there is a road net established. The best way to transport water in cold regions involves using tracked vehicles that do not depend on a road for maneuverability. If units use 5-gallon (19-liter) cans to carry water, they fill the cans only three-quarters full to allow agitation of the water during transit. Troops store cans off the floor in heated shelters as soon as delivered. Sled-mounted 250 to 300 gallon (946 to 1,135 liters) water tanks on which troops have installed immersion-type heaters have proven satisfactory.

5-26. For small units of two to four men, an insulated 5-gallon food container is satisfactory. Troops can fill these each night with water from melted snow or ice or from unit water dispensers. Each container holds enough water for the minimum daily needs of about four men. The container's insulation keeps water from freezing for as long as 40 hours at an ambient temperature of -20 °F (-29°C), if the temperature of the water was at the boiling point when filling the container.

5-27. Disposing of waste water proves a constant problem in extreme cold and, even in the summer, in the presence of underlying permafrost. For periods of up to 6 months, units can construct satisfactory drains by digging or blasting deep pits, filling these pits with large rocks, and then re-covering the pits with about 1.5 inches (50 centimeters) of earth.

Class II

5-28. Requirements for clothing, individual equipment, and shelter increase for operations conducted in cold region environments. To the largest extent possible, troops store class II items at the company and battalion level. Severe cold requires a large number of tents for many purposes, to include the warming of personnel, mess activities, maintenance operations, and critical supply storage. Class II items have a high priority for movement since they support the operational force and ensure its survival.

Class III

5-29. The consumption of fuel may be so great that supplying a modular brigade can require up to one-half of the total cargo capacity of supporting transportation units. Soldiers and Marines must start vehicles frequently to prevent cold-soaking of engines and power trains. Since vehicles must use lower gears to traverse unimproved roads and snow-covered ground, fuel consumption can increase by as much as 25 percent. Vehicles use large amounts of fuel for heaters to keep personnel and sensitive equipment warm. To ensure survival of the force, movement of fuel must have a high priority. Units need to maintain fuel reserves at each echelon to guard against interruptions in resupply operations.

Class IV

5-30. The brigade support battalion provides class IV to its supported brigade combat team (BCT) and to other units operating in the BCT area of operations on an area basis when possible. Non-BCT units may require class IV resupply from the sustainment brigade. If possible, support units carry additional quantities of class IV since troops construct fighting positions above ground due to the permafrost.

Class V

5-31. Units need to keep ammunition on hand. They may establish pre-designated levels of on-hand quantities and restrict firing when they reach these levels. Like in any operation, units make every effort to keep the basic load on hand to guard against interruption in resupply operations.

5-32. Fires units typically consume large volumes of ammunition and require continuous resupply to support combat operations. To facilitate this end, units can load ammunition by type on supporting unit vehicles to provide for rapid movement when called forward by the fires unit. However, this method may tie up critically needed transportation assets. Instead, units can tailgate ammunition from support vehicles to unit vehicles at mobile supply points. The preferred method of resupply travels by throughput shipments directly from the point of entry into the combat area or the ammunition supply point to the firing battalion.

5-33. Whenever possible, troops use vehicles to resupply units. When wheeled vehicles can reach units, units use mobile supply units and tailgating. Deep snow and limited trafficability may force units to use other methods, such as tracked vehicles or even carrying by hand to resupply ammunition. Units use aviation assets to aid in the movement of ammunition, but this is limited by weather and the air defense capability of the enemy.

Class VI

5-34. Personal items receive the lowest priority of movement while units conduct offensive and defensive combat operations in the cold region environment. Extended LOCs, limited transportation assets, and the increased use of supplies limit the availability of class VI. Leaders can make class VI available by placing class VI items with rations whenever possible. However, when the nature of the conflict turns to stability or civil support operations, class VI supplies take on a much higher priority.

Class VII

5-35. The requirement for major end items depends on the intensity and duration of the conflict. Leaders emphasize maintenance and repair rather than item replacement. Class VII items are intensely managed and controlled through command channels. When they become available, the quartermaster support company in the sustainment brigade or from the strategic level distributes these items to the brigade support battalion distribution company.

Class VIII

5-36. Units give medical supplies a high priority for movement and move them by air whenever possible. Normally medical items require heated transportation since they are particularly susceptible to damage from freezing. The following items are particularly vulnerable to the cold:
- Oxygen or compressed gas tanks.
- Surgical sinks.
- X-Ray machines.
- Combat lifesaver bag contents.
- Medications, intravenous solutions, and especially whole blood.

Class IX

5-37. Severe cold, rough unimproved roads, snow, and rugged terrain will probably increase repair parts requirements during operations in cold region environments. Leaders emphasize operator-level maintenance. Units should carry and hold parts with high-usage factors as far forward as possible to speed repair of equipment. Whenever possible, unit maintenance leaders adjust prescribed load lists before deployment so the unit can carry more high-demand parts on hand.

MAINTENANCE

5-38. Initial evaluation of the nature and extent of the damage is instrumental to rapid repair in cold region environments. When the operator makes a good evaluation, then unit maintenance personnel or supporting units can dispatch the right personnel, the right tools, and repair parts. Operators and maintenance teams need to familiarize themselves with FM 4-30.31 since it covers rapid battle damage assessment and repair.

5-39. Preventative maintenance checks and services (PMCS) take on special importance in cold region environments. Effective PMCS greatly reduces the workload of unit maintenance personnel and ensures operational readiness rates remain high. See table 5-1 on page 5-6 for general techniques when operating in the cold region environment that help prevent breakage.

Table 5-1. Techniques to prevent breakage

Focus	Technique
Engine	Operate vehicles periodically to prevent cold-soaking of engines and power trains.
	Keep all types of batteries fully warmed and fully charged.
	Keep machine surfaces clean at all times.
	Perform as much maintenance as possible to avoid overwhelming the capabilities of supporting units.
Fuel	Add icing inhibitors to fuel.
	Minimize condensation of moisture inside fuel tanks by refilling immediately after stopping.
	Keep fuel tanks at least one-quarter full.
Interior	Keep optical instruments from undergoing sudden and extreme changes in temperatures when possible.
	Realize that windshields crack easily when subjected to sudden blasts of warm air.
Lubrication	Winterize equipment according to the appropriate equipment lube order and technical manuals.
	If lubrication is needed, lubricate immediately after operating the vehicle while parts are warm. This ensures maximum penetration of lubricants.
	Keep stored lubricants warm.
	Apply lubrication according to the temperature range of the equipment lube order.
	Complete daily checks to ensure that water or antifreeze is not present in crankcase oil. If detected, determine the cause immediately and change out the oil.
Safety	Resist the tendency to operate equipment in a closed area to avoid carbon monoxide poisoning.
Wheels	Realize that links are stiff when cold and should not be forced.
	Choke wheels instead of setting the hand brake. This prevents the brakes from freezing.
	Park vehicles on timber, brush, or any other material that will keep tires or tracks from freezing to the ground.
	Cap tire stems.

PERSONNEL SERVICES

5-40. Units screen personnel medical records for specific medical conditions before deployment. While these conditions do not necessarily prevent deployment, these troops are deemed as a high risk:

- Circulatory diseases affecting the extremities.
- Skin grafts on the face or neck area.
- Chronic inner-ear medical problems.
- Previous cold injuries.

5-41. Cold region environments demand that replacements be properly equipped and indoctrinated prior to joining units in the field. Whenever possible, units conduct training in areas that parallel the area of operations and include a period of acclimatization before deploying to the combat area. These efforts will reduce the chance of these new personnel becoming casualties due to lack of inexperience or training.

5-42. The theater sustainment command executes mortuary affairs activities through the sustainment brigades. Remains will not deteriorate as quickly in the cold region environment, but units evacuate them as soon as practically possible by air means.

MEDICAL PLANS

5-43. While preparing the medical support plan, all medical units consider the tactical commander's plan. Medical units must be able to rapidly adjust to changes in the situation and be just as mobile as the supported unit. Commanders place units as far forward as possible to reduce how long patients wait in the cold while being evacuated. Troops defer definitive treatment needs to role II medical units located at the brigade support battalion or higher. In forward areas, troop medics should only perform procedures that will stabilize and prepare the patient for evacuation.

5-44. Because of the combined effects of severe cold and shock, units evacuate patients by the quickest means possible. Units need to keep air evacuation as the primary means of evacuation and accomplish it as far forward as the tactical situation and weather permit.

5-45. If a unit experiences multiple casualties in a short period, medics can be overwhelmed. Often times, landing zones that are under fire prevent or delay casualty evacuation. Cold region environments often exacerbate problems with weather, terrain, high altitude, and frequency modulated (commonly known as FM) radios. Combined with enemy fire, these problems delay even the best-laid plans to evacuate casualties. These factors will increase the need for on-the-spot medical help.

This page intentionally left blank.

Chapter 6

Applying Combat Power in Cold Regions

Commanders conceptualize capabilities in terms of combat power. The eight elements of combat power consist of leadership, information, movement and maneuver, intelligence, fires, sustainment, command and control, and protection. Leadership and information are applied through, and multiply the effects of, the other six elements of combat power. These six—movement and maneuver, intelligence, fires, sustainment, command and control, and protection—are collectively described as the warfighting functions. The cold region environment impacts the warfighting functions in unique ways. No matter the environment, units will execute many processes in the same manner.

LEADERSHIP

6-1. The cold region environment affects leaders and their ability to lead. Because they are human, they are susceptible to the cold like their troops. The traits, qualities, and abilities requisite to good leadership in any theater of operations assume their greatest importance during offensive operations in cold region environments. Leaders must be impressed with and made clearly aware of this fact. Without proper training, leadership, and discipline, few Soldiers or Marines will be able to meet the rigid standards and the difficult service required of operations in cold region environment.

6-2. First, leaders need to be aware of their cocoon-like existence. This occurs when Soldiers and Marines, bundled up in layers of clothing with the head covered by a hood, tend to withdraw within themselves. Such clothing tends to restrict an individual's hearing and field of vision and the individual becomes oblivious to the surroundings. Leaders must recognize these symptoms in their troops and themselves. Leaders stay alert to prevent the growth of lethargy. By appearing alert to their troops, leaders also prevent troops from sinking into a state of cocoon existence. One method leaders use to stay alert involves throwing back their hoods and engaging in physical activity. Not only does this reenergize the mind, it produces warmth as well.

6-3. Often Soldiers and Marines suffer from individual or group hibernation in cold region environments. This process again manifests from withdrawal from the surrounding environment. Afflicted individuals tend to seek the comfort of sleeping bags. Afflicted groups remain in tents or other shelters while neglecting their duties. In the offense, troops often stay in vehicles due to the continued motion of the battle that hinders the use of shelters. In extreme cases, troops may abandon guard and security measures jeopardizing the safety of the unit. Leaders ensure all personnel remain alert and active. They rigidly insist that troops properly execute their military duties and promptly and properly perform their group duties.

MOVEMENT AND MANEUVER

6-4. Chapter 3 covers specific details of movement and maneuver. It discusses how the cold region environment affects movement and maneuver by individuals, vehicles, and aircraft.

INTELLIGENCE

6-5. Chapter 1 describes the key terrain, light data, and climatic considerations. Understanding situational awareness and targeting requires leaders to consider how the cold affects intelligence, surveillance, and reconnaissance (ISR) activities. Leaders gain this understanding by conducting effective intelligence preparation of the battlefield.

6-6.   In a cold environment, Soldiers and Marines often experience problems using sensors described in paragraphs 3-143 through 3-144. Therefore, they use a robust defensive plan incorporating several listening posts and observation posts in key terrain. Once units identify enemy forces, they can employ the reserve effectively. When positioning troops in defensive positions, leaders consider the temperature and wind chill, especially when temperatures reach -40 °F (-40 °C) or below. Soldiers and Marines can only tolerate these conditions for short periods.

TERRAIN AND WEATHER CONSIDERATIONS

6-7.   Units control existing lines of communications (LOCs) to ensure success in a cold region environment. Severe winter weather hastens enemy destruction after units cut enemy LOCs. Units breach enemy LOCs near dominating terrain if the unit must retain the area. During the summer, leaders select such objectives where the LOCs cross a river or pass between two existing natural obstacles.

CONDUCTING INTELLIGENCE, SURVEILLANCE, AND RECONNAISSANCE

6-8.   ISR synchronizes and integrates the planning and operation of sensors, assets, and processing, exploitation, and dissemination systems in direct support of current and future operations. For Army forces, this activity is a combined arms operation that focuses on priority intelligence requirements while answering the commander's critical information requirements. The cold presents unique opportunities and challenges when conducting ISR. Table 6-1 on page 6-3 lists imagery sensors, their descriptions, and the advantages and disadvantages that climate places upon them.

6-9.   Units need to include engineers and field artillery assets in reconnaissance and surveillance missions. In cold regions, units often need bridging or rafting equipment to conduct reconnaissance and surveillance missions. To maintain momentum, planners identify the need for this equipment and select bridging, fording, or rafting sites as early as possible in the operation. Along these lines, units place engineer units and special equipment as far forward as possible.

FIRES

6-10. If units employ fires, a period of slow movement may occur between the cessation of field artillery fire on the enemy forward positions and the arrival of the infantry on the objective. Planners consider this period of slow movement caused by terrain or weather conditions when planning fire support of the assault. However, when terrain, weather, and lack of effective enemy resistance permits, mechanized infantry may remain in their carriers and make a mounted assault. This assault capitalizes on the shock effect and reduces the time lag associated with a dismounted assault through snow and underbrush.

6-11. Commanders analyze movement requirements for fires units to support the maneuver force. Rearming and refueling will require attention. Depending on the availability of air and ground resupply assets, commanders may need to deploy with lighter but more mobile and supportable artillery. Vehicles such as the small unit support vehicle can then transport light artillery.

6-12. Deep snow and mud reduce fragmentation effects of artillery, mortars, and hand grenades using point detonating (PD) fuses. Greater use of alternate fusing such as variable time or proximity improves weapons effects against exposed targets. PD fuses remain effective against improved positions; the great durability of positions in frozen ground may make employing precision munitions highly desirable. Frozen and stone-covered ground greatly improves the fragmentation since the terrain produces secondary fragmentation.

6-13. Deep soft snow may not provide sufficient resistance to cause PD fuses to activate. As little as 6 inches of snow can smother PD rounds, reducing their bursting effectiveness by as much as 80 percent. Soft ground, mud, and muskeg can have a similar effect. Units can normally solve these problems by using more variable time (VT) fuses; however, some VT fuses malfunction at temperatures below 0 °F (-18 °C) and in heavy rain or snow. Whenever possible, units store fuses in a warm place prior to use. Special considerations apply to phosphorus shells. These shells produce the desired smoke effect, but they can contaminate the area of impact with phosphorus particles that remain buried in the snow.

Table 6-1. Sensor characteristics

Sensor	Description	Advantages	Disadvantages
Visible (Optical)	• Best tool for daytime, clear weather, detailed analysis. Includes video and electro-optical.	• Affords a familiar view of a scene. • Offers system resolution that cannot be achieved in other optical systems or in thermal images and radars. • Offers detailed analysis and measurements. • Offers stereoscopic viewing.	• Is restricted by terrain and vegetation. • Is limited to daytime use only. • Creates reduced picture size.
Infrared	• Best tool for nighttime, clear weather, detailed analysis. Includes overhead nonimaging infrared.	• Has a passive sensor and is impossible to jam. • Offers camouflage penetration. • Provides good resolution. • Has nighttime imaging capability.	• Is not effective during thermal crossover periods. • Is not easily interpretable. • Requires skilled analysis. • Cannot penetrate clouds.
Radar	• Useful tool for detecting presence of objects at night and in bad weather. Includes synthetic aperture radar coherent change detection and multi-spectral thermal imaging.	• Can be used in all weather; can penetrate fog, haze, clouds, and smoke. • Can be used in day or night. • Does not rely on visible light nor thermal radiation. • Has good standoff capability. • Covers a large area. • Allows moving target detection. • Penetrates foliage and ground.	• Is not easily interpretable. • Requires skilled analysis. • Is inhibited by terrain masking.
Multi-Spectral Imagery	• Best tool for mapping purposes and terrain analysis.	• Has a large database available. • Can manipulate band combinations to display desired requirements. • Can merge images with other digital data to provide higher resolution.	• Is not easily interpretable. • Requires skilled analysis. • Requires manipulating a computer that uses large amounts of memory and storage and processing capabilities.

6-14. Because of slower burning rates for propellants, maximum effective ranges for artillery may be reduced by a kilometer. Initial rounds fired from cold tubes also have reduced range. For these reasons, Soldiers and Marines must use caution when firing initial adjustment rounds.

6-15. During the winter season, shortened daylight hours limit opportunities for visual adjustment of fires. In windless extreme cold conditions, ice fog and lingering smoke may limit observation. If snow obscures terrain features, troops may find determining the range more difficult. Snow and mud may conceal the impact of an artillery round; units can adjust using low airburst or smoke. Commanders remind Soldiers and Marines of the affects of looming on range estimation.

SUSTAINMENT

6-16. Chapter 5 covered details of sustainment for all classes of supply. However, offensive operations involve considerable expenditure of ammunition, petroleum, oil, and lubricants. Units ensure they are supplied to the fullest extent possible before engaging in combat operations in a cold region environment. Due to the extended LOCs and the chance of attack along these extended lines, leaders develop robust protection for ground convoys. FM 4-01.45 discusses techniques for effective convoy security.

COMMAND AND CONTROL

6-17. Commanders combine the art of command and the science of control to accomplish missions in a cold region environment. Characteristics of the cold region environment hinder command and control by hindering communications between the commander and troops.

6-18. All units and personnel must maintain personal communication and contact. Due to the normal deadening of the senses, a lone individual may quickly become oblivious to the surroundings. Commanders keep each individual and group informed of what is happening. Commanders take strong measures to ensure that each small-unit leader keeps subordinates informed. General information has value, but commanders place the greatest importance on matters of immediate concern and interest to the individual.

6-19. Command and control and the ability to coordinate prove extremely important in the cold region environment when conducting offensive operations. At certain times, the distance between two attacking forces may become so great that troops must relay messages. Planners need to consider the key terrain that units must capture to set up potential relay sites.

6-20. As in all operations, commanders inform their staff officers as early as possible of all aspects for conducting the attack. Then planners can issue fragmentary and operation orders as far in advance as possible. This notification takes on particular importance in the cold region environment since everything takes longer to coordinate and to make preparations. This applies especially to the S-4 or G-4 whose arrangements for logistic support often require additional time.

PROTECTION

6-21. Protecting the force includes protecting personnel, physical assets, and information. In a cold region environment, this protection applies to that from the enemy as well as the environment. Chapter 3 discusses how to protect personnel whereas chapters 4 and 5 discuss how to protect equipment.

6-22. Protection of the force includes protection from enemy attacks. Leaders and planners consider how much of the force to allocate to the attack. Even with robust engineer support, the limited road networks limit which routes leaders and staffs use in cold regions. Roads are easily identifiable on maps, forces will be spread thin, and the LOCs will be extended. These factors easily enable the enemy to conduct attacks to disable the road network and prevent resupply. Therefore, commanders keep a force that can provide a robust defense in place to protect against an attack at likely points. Planners place special emphasis on protecting air defense considering the importance that air supremacy has in cold region environments.

6-23. Often the cold region environment makes identifying friendly forces from enemy forces problematic. Both forces will be wearing white camouflage. Therefore, units enforce a system that changes daily but stays simple enough for Soldiers and Marines to remember. Suggestions include using white or multicolored tape on individuals and using colored flags on vehicles. Troops need to avoid attaching these markers to antennas since it will degrade their performance. Lastly, Soldiers and Marines must thoroughly understand and be familiar with enemy and friendly vehicles and equipment.

6-24. The United States does not use chemical weapons in offensive operations (see FM 3-11 for a discussion of chemical weapons). Therefore, the Army only maintains a defensive posture to counter any enemy force that might employ such weapons while engaging American forces. Leaders, Soldiers, and Marines reference FM 3-11.4 for techniques and procedures on chemical, biological, radiological, and nuclear protection in cold region environments. In addition, FM 3-11.9 describes some environmental considerations that affect chemical and biological agents that enemy forces use.

6-25. The cold region environment does not change Army procedures for protecting information or operational security. When revised, FM 3-13 will address information protection. Marines refer to MCWP 3-40.2. It discusses force health protection issues in depth in chapter 3. Personnel, such as pilots, who have an increased likelihood of being isolated refer to FM 3-50.3 and FM 3-05.70. Marines refer to MCWP 4-11.1 for health service support.

Appendix A

Army Cold Weather Uniform and Equipment Posture

This appendix discusses uniforms and equipment used by Army forces in cold region environments. This appendix does not apply to Marine Corps personnel. Marines refer to MCRP 3-35.1A.

Note: The use or mention of any commercial or private organization's name or trademark and the organization's services or funds by the Army or Marine Corps does not express or imply an endorsement of the sponsor or its products and services by the Army or Marine Corps.

A-1. The tables on pages A-2 through A-6 are recommendations for Soldiers based on temperature ranges they encounter in cold regions. These recommendations cover clothing, equipment, training, nutrition, shelter and heat sources, and other additional control measures. Table A-1 covers the temperature ranging from 55 °F (13 °C) to 33 °F (0 °C).

Table A-1.Temperature zone 1: 55 °F (15 °C) to 33 °F (0 °C)

Area of Consideration	Special Requirements and Recommended Actions		
Available Personal Clothing and Equipment	Clothing Layer:	ECWCS Generation II	ECWCS Generation III
	Base layer	• Lightweight polypropylene top and bottom and/or • Midweight polypropylene top and bottom	• Lightweight cold weather undershirt and drawers and/or • Midweight cold weather shirt/drawers
	Insulating layer	• Shirt, cold weather, black fleece and/or • Liner, cold weather, coat	• Green fleece jacket
	Outer shell	• Generation II GORE-TEX® jacket • Generation II GORE-TEX® trousers	• Wind cold weather jacket (wind shirt) • Extreme cold/wet weather jacket (hard shell) • Extreme cold/wet weather trousers (hard shell)
	Other: • Issued GORE-TEX® gloves with liners • Issued wool socks with synthetic liner sock • Temperate boots; cold weather boots recommended (Belleville 795, Danner Ft. Lewis 400g Tan Military Boots)		• Balaclava and neck gaiter • Suspenders • Knife • Arctic necklace (lighter and lip balm worn around neck)
Training	• Knowledge of cold region environmental hazards • Knowledge of cold weather clothing capabilities and limitations • Skill to use cold weather clothing and equipment to provide protection from the elements • Skill to prevent, recognize, and treat cold injuries		
Food and Water	• Meals ready to eat • One hot meal daily as mission dictates • 3.5–5 quarts of water per day • Water filter (recommend: first need portable water filter)		
Shelter and Heat	• Patrol bag • GORE-TEX® bivouac cover • Sleeping mat • Poncho • Poncho liner (optional)		
Additional Control Measures	• Water re-supply plan • Sanitation plan		

A-2.   Table A-2 covers the temperature ranging from 32 °F (0 °C) to 14 °F (-10 °C).

Table A-2.Temperature zone 2: 32 °F (0 °C) to 14 °F (-10 °C)

Area of Consideration	Special Requirements and Recommended Actions		
	Clothing Layer:	ECWCS Generation II	ECWCS Generation III
Available Personal Clothing and Equipment	Base layer	• Polypropylene undershirt and drawers • Drawers cold weather, polyester, brown lightweight undershirt and drawers	• Lightweight cold weather undershirt and drawers • Midweight cold weather shirt/drawers
	Insulating layer	• Shirt and overalls, cold weather, black fleece and/or • Liner, cold weather, coat and trousers	• Green fleece jacket
	Outer shell	• Generation II GORE-TEX® jacket • Generation II GORE-TEX® trousers	• Wind cold weather jacket (wind shirt) • Extreme cold/wet weather jacket (hard shell) • Extreme cold/wet weather trousers (hard shell) • Extreme cold weather parka (puffy Jacket)
	Other: • Issued GORE-TEX® gloves with liners • Issued wool socks with synthetic liner sock • Cold weather boots (Belleville 795, Danner Ft. Lewis 400g Tan Military Boots) • Arctic necklace (lighter and lip balm worn around neck)		• Trigger finger mittens with extra trigger finger liners • Suspenders • Contact gloves • Knife • Balaclava and neck gaiter • Ski goggles
Training	Northern Warfare Training Center Arctic Light Individual Training Program or similar program		
Food and Water	• Meal, cold weather (MCW) 1 bag = 1 meal which provides about 1500 calories • 34 ounces of heated water are required to hydrate one MCW • 2 hot meals per day as mission dictates		• 3.5–5 quarts of water per day • 1 stove per team to heat water for rations and/or melt snow for water
Shelter and Heat	Individual: • MSS, all components • Sleeping mat, poncho and poncho liner		Squad: • Ahkio group complete (see appendix B) • Arctic 10-man tent • Space heater arctic
Additional Control Measures	• Begin leader/medic checks for cold injuries; 2-3 times daily at minimum • Water re-supply and storage plan (to prevent water from freezing) • Sanitation plan • No skin camouflage below 32 °F (0 °C)		• Contact gloves must be worn when working outdoors • POL gloves must be worn when working with fuel • Consider four-season, 2-4 man shelters for personnel that work away from support base
MSS medium shelter system		POL petroleum, oil, and lubricants	

A-3. Table A-3 covers the temperature ranging from 14 °F (-10 °C) to -19 °F (-28 °C).

Table A-3. Temperature zone 3: 14 °F (-10 °C) to -19 °F (-28 °C)

Area of Consideration	Special Requirements and Recommended Actions		
Available Personal Clothing and Equipment	Clothing Layer:	ECWCS Generation II	ECWCS Generation III
	Base layer	• Polypropylene undershirt and drawers • Drawers cold weather, polyester, brown lightweight undershirt and drawers	• Lightweight cold weather undershirt and drawers • Midweight cold weather shirt/drawers
	Insulating layer	• Shirt and overalls, cold weather, black fleece and/or • Liner, cold weather, coat and trousers	• Green fleece jacket
	Outer shell	• Generation II GORE-TEX® jacket and • Generation II GORE-TEX® trousers	• Wind cold weather jacket (wind shirt) • Soft shell cold weather jacket (soft shell) • Soft shell cold weather trousers (soft shell) • Extreme cold weather parka (puffy jacket) • Extreme cold weather trousers
	Other: • Suspenders • Issued wool socks with synthetic liner sock • Cold weather boots (Belleville 795, Danner Ft. Lewis 400g Tan Military Boot) for short duration outdoor work • White vapor barrier boots • Trigger finger mittens with extra TF liners		• Contact gloves • Issued GORE-TEX® gloves with liners • Balaclava and neck gaiter • Arctic mittens • Knife • Arctic necklace (lighter and lip balm worn around neck) • Ski goggles
Training	• Northern Warfare Training Center Arctic Light Individual Training Program or similar program		
Food and Water	• Meal, cold weather (MCW) 1 bag = 1 meal which provides about 1500 calories • 34 ounces of heated water are required to hydrate one MCW • 2 hot meals per day as mission dictates		• 3.5–5 quarts of water per day • 1 stove per team to heat water for rations and/or melt snow for water
Shelter and Heat	Individual: • MSS, all components • Sleeping mat, poncho and poncho liner		Squad: • Ahkio group complete (see appendix B) • Arctic 10-man tent • Space heater arctic
Additional Control Measures	• Implement all control measures from Temperature zone 2 and change/add: • Increase frequency of leader/medic checks for cold injuries • Rotate Soldiers in static positions frequently		• Provide warm tents and/or vehicles for Soldiers • Provide four-season shelters for personnel that work away from support base
MSS medium shelter system			

A-4. Table A-4 covers the temperature ranging from -20 °F (-29 °C) to -40 °F (-40 °C).

Table A-4.Temperature zone 4: -20 °F (-29 °C) to -40 °F (-40 °C)

Area of Consideration	Special Requirements and Recommended Actions		
Available Personal Clothing and Equipment	Clothing Layer:	ECWCS Generation II	ECWCS Generation III
	Base layer	• Polypropylene undershirt and drawers • Drawers cold weather, polyester, brown lightweight undershirt and drawers	• Lightweight cold weather undershirt and drawers • Midweight cold weather shirt/drawers
	Insulating layer	• Shirt and overalls, cold weather, black fleece and/or • Liner, cold weather, coat and trousers	• Green fleece jacket
	Outer shell	• Generation II GORE-TEX® jacket • Generation II GORE-TEX® trousers	• Wind cold weather jacket (wind shirt) • Soft shell cold weather jacket (soft shell) • Soft shell cold weather trousers (soft shell) • Extreme cold weather parka (puffy jacket) • Extreme cold weather trousers
	Other: • Suspenders • Issued wool socks with synthetic liner sock • Cold weather boots (Belleville 795, Danner Ft. Lewis 400g Tan Military Boot) for short duration outdoor work • Black or white vapor barrier boots in the field • Balaclava and neck gaiter		• Contact gloves • Issued GORE-TEX® gloves with liners • Trigger finger mittens with extra TF liners • Arctic mittens • Knife • Arctic necklace (lighter and lip balm worn around neck) • Ski goggles
Training	Northern Warfare Training Center Arctic Light Individual Training Program or similar program		
Food and Water	• Meal, cold weather (MCW) 1 bag = 1 meal which provides about 1500 calories • 34 ounces of heated water are required to hydrate one MCW • 2 hot meals per day as mission dictates		• 3.5–5 quarts of water per day • 1 stove per team to heat water for rations and/or melt snow for water
Shelter and Heat	Individual: • MSS, all components • Sleeping mat, poncho and poncho liner		Squad: • Ahkio group complete (see appendix B) • Arctic 10-man tent • Space heater arctic
Additional Control Measures	• Implement all control measures from Temperature zone 3 and change/add: • Limit outdoor operations and training; closely scrutinize operations and training by leaders		• Perform hourly leader/medic checks for cold injuries • Recognize risk level is high • Cover all exposed skin • Avoid static duty
MSS medium shelter system			

A-5. Table A-5 covers the temperature ranging below -40 °F (-40 °C).

Table A-5.Temperature zone 5: Below -40 °F (-40 °C)

Area of Consideration	Special Requirements and Recommended Actions		
Available Personal Clothing and Equipment	Clothing Layer:	ECWCS Generation II	ECWCS Generation III
	Base layer	• Polypropylene undershirt and drawers • Drawers cold weather, polyester, brown lightweight undershirt and drawers	• Lightweight cold weather undershirt and drawers and/or • Midweight cold weather shirt/drawers
	Insulating layer	• Shirt and overalls, cold weather, black fleece and/or • Liner, cold weather, coat and trousers	• Green fleece jacket
	Outer shell	• Generation II GORE-TEX® jacket • Generation II GORE-TEX® trousers	• Wind cold weather jacket (wind shirt) • Soft shell cold weather jacket (soft shell) • Soft shell cold weather trousers (soft shell) • Extreme cold weather parka (puffy jacket) • Extreme cold weather trousers
	Other: • Suspenders • Issued wool socks with synthetic liner sock • Cold weather boots (Belleville 795, Danner Ft. Lewis 400g Tan Military Boot) for short duration outdoor work • Black or white vapor barrier boots in the field		• Contact gloves • Issued GORE-TEX® gloves with liners • Trigger finger mittens with extra TF liners • Arctic mittens • Knife • Arctic necklace (lighter and lip balm worn around neck) • Balaclava and neck gaiter
Training	Northern Warfare Training Center Arctic Light Individual Training Program or similar program		
Food and Water	• Meal, cold weather (MCW) 1 bag = 1 meal which provides about 1500 calories • 34 ounces of heated water are required to hydrate one MCW	• 3.5–5 quarts of water per day • 2 hot meals per day as mission dictates • 1 stove per team to heat water for rations and/or melt snow for water	
Shelter and Heat	Individual: • MSS, all components • sleeping mat, poncho and poncho liner	Squad: • Ahkio group complete (see appendix B) • Arctic 10-man tent • Space heater arctic	
Additional Control Measures	• Implement all control measures from Temperature zone 4 and change/add: • Recognize risk level is extremely high	• Limit outdoor operations and training to critical life support tasks only • Warm tents and/or vehicles for all personnel	
MSS medium shelter system			

Appendix B

Army Compatible Heaters and Tents

This appendix discusses the space heaters and tents used by Army forces in cold region environments. Fires teams working in a cold region of 32 °F (0 °C) and below should use a small stove such as the MSR® Whisperlite Internationale or MSR® XGK-EX. Marines refer to MCRP 3-35.1A for stoves and tents.

Note: The use or mention of any commercial or private organization's name or trademark and the organization's services or funds by the Army or Marine Corps does not express or imply an endorsement of the sponsor or its products and services by the Army or Marine Corps.

B-1.   Table B-1 lists available space heaters for the cold region environment. The table includes not only a picture of the space heater, but its detailed name, stock number, dimensions, weight, and output.

Table B-1. Heater descriptions

Item	Description	Item	Description
	Space Heater Small 4520-01-478-9207 16"L x 9"W x 14"H 32 pounds 12,000 BTU/Hr		Heater, Tent (UH68ODH) PN 168325 30"L x 11"W x 24"H 125 pounds 60,000 BTU/Hr 110 VAC, 450 Watts
	Space Heater Arctic 4520-01-444-2375 17"L x 9"W x 17"H 41 pounds 25,000 BTU/Hr		Large Capacity Field Heater 4520-01-500-1534 62"L x 40"H x 44.5"W 622 pounds 400,000 BTU/Hr Self-Powered, Diesel Engine
	H45 Space Heater 4520-01-329-3451 18" diameter x 24" H 65 pounds 45,000 BTU/Hr		Multi-fuel Tent Heater (MTH150) PN 15000 56"L x 26"W x 31"H 200 pounds 120,000 BTU/Hr 110 VAC, 12 amps

Table B-1. Heater descriptions, cont.

Item	Description	Item	Description
	Space Heater Convective (SHC 35) 4520-01-431-8927 40"L x 14"W x 18"H 74 pounds 35,000 BTU/Hr Self-Powered		CBRNE Multi-fuel Tent Heater (MTH150CP) PN 15000-1 56"L x 26"W x 31"H 200 pounds 120,000 BTU/Hr 110 VAC, 12 amps
	Space Heater Convective (SHC 60) 4520-01-520-6477 44 ¾"L x 17"H x19"W 98 pounds 60,000 BTU/Hr Self-Powered		MV60S-1 Space Heater PN 53457-1 51"L x 16.5"W x 25"H 115 pounds 60,000 BTU/Hr 110VAC, 4.75 amps
	UH68G1 Space Heater 4520-01-203-4410 26"L x 22"H x 10"W 110 pounds 60,000 BTU/Hr 110 VAC, 450 Watts		A20 Space Heater/CBH 4250-01-396-2826 27"L x 8"diameter 38 pounds 60,000 BTU/Hr 24 VDC, 20 amps

B-2. Tables B-2 and B-3 list the different shelters available. Table B-2 lists the smaller shelters whereas table B-3 lists the larger shelters. These tables include the abbreviated name of each shelter, a brief description, and the floor dimensions. Tables B-4 and B-5 reference the abbreviated names.

Table B-2. Shelter specifications

Shelter type	Abbreviated name	Floor dimensions (total square feet)
Soldier Crew Tent	SCT	10' x 10' 100 sq. ft
Five Man Arctic	5 Man Arctic	8'9" octagon 200 sq. ft
Ten Man Arctic	10 Man Arctic	17'6" x 17'6" 306 sq. ft.
Modular Command Post System	MCPS	11' x 11' 121 sq. ft
Modular General Purpose Tent System, Medium	MGPTS Medium	36' x 18' 648 sq. ft
Modular General Purpose Tent System, Small	MGPTS Small	18' x 18' 324 sq. ft
Tent, General Purpose, Medium	GP Medium	32' x 16' 512 sq. ft
Tent, General Purpose, Small	GP Small	17'6" x 17'6" 306 sq. ft.
Small Shelter System	SSS	20' x 32' 650 sq. ft
Tent, Extendable Modular Personnel	TEMPER	32' x 20' 640 sq. ft
Base-X Expeditionary Shelter	305	18' x 25' 450 sq. ft.
ft feet sq square		

Table B-3. Large shelter specifications

Shelter type	Abbreviated name	Floor dimensions (total square feet)
Modular General Purpose Tent System, Large	MGPTS Large	18' x 54' 972 sq. ft
Medium Shelter System	MSS	52' x 29.5' 1500 sq. ft
Lightweight Maintenance Enclosure	LME	32' x 25' 800 sq. ft
Base-X Expeditionary Shelter, (TOC, UOC)	6D31 Dome	27' x 31' 615 sq. ft.
ft feet sq square		

B-3. Table B-4 lists the heater types that heat the smaller shelter types. Refer to tables B-2 and B-3 for source of abbreviated names. In table B-4, the number 1 means that one heater will suffice to heat that particular shelter. The number 2 means that two heaters are required to heat that particular shelter.

Table B-4. Heaters needed by small shelter

Application	SCT	5 and 10 man Arctic	MCPS	MGPTS Small	MGPTS Medium	GP Medium	GP Small	SSS	TEMPER Tent	305
Space Heater Small	1									
Space Heater Arctic		1								
H45			2	1		2		2	2	1
SHC 35			1	1		2	1	2	2	1
SHC 60			1	1		1	1	1	1	1
UH68ODH			1	1		1	1	1	1	1
MV60S-1			1	1		1	1	1	1	1
MTH150					1			1	1	
MTH150CP					1			1	1	

B-4. Larger shelters consist of tents, hard shelters, and vehicles. Table B-5 lists the heater types that heat the larger and mobile shelter types. Refer to tables B-2 and B-3 for source of abbreviated names.

Table B-5. Large types of shelter and their heaters

Application	MGPTS Large	MSS	LME	6D31 Dome	CBRN	Expansible Van Body	Hard Wall Shelter	Cargo	Vehicle
Large Capacity Field Heater	X	X	X	X					
MTH150CP	X	X	X	X	X				
A20 / CBH					X		X	X	X
UH68G1						X	X	X	

Source Notes

These are the sources used or paraphrased in this publication. They are listed by page number. Where material appears in a paragraph, both page and paragraph number are listed.

v   "When conducting military operations …": Swinzow, George K. *On Winter Warfare. Special Report 93-12*. United States Army Cold Regions Research and Engineering Laboratory, Hanover, New Hampshire, June 1993.

1-2   para 1-4, "The subarctic is the …": *Test Operations Procedure (TOP) 1-1-017 Cold Regions Environmental Considerations*. United States Army Cold Regions Test Center, Delta Junction, Alaska, 22 September 2008.

4-5   para 4-30, "Vehicle operation on freezing …": Shoop, S. , G. Koenig, and P. Richmond. *Vehicle Trafficability of Freezing and Thawing Ground Conditions: Engineer Research and Development Center/United States Army Cold Regions Research and Engineering Laboratory Letter Report LR-10-10*. United States Army Cold Regions Research and Engineering Laboratory, Hanover, New Hampshire, August 2001.

4-7   para 4-36, "Often, a conventional gravel…": Kestler, M., S. Shoop, K. Henry, J. Stark, and R. Affleck. *Rapid Stabilization of Thawing Soils for Enhanced Vehicle Mobility. United States Army Cold Regions Research and Engineering Laboratory Report 99-3*, Hanover, New Hampshire, February 1999.

4-10   para 4-53, "Because chemical reactions proceed …": Diemand, Deborah and James H. Lever. *Cold Regions Issues for Off-Road Autonomous Vehicles: Engineer Research and Development Center/United States Army Cold Regions Research and Engineering Laboratory Technical Report TR-04-6*, Hanover, New Hampshire, April 2004.

This page intentionally left blank.

Glossary

ACL	authorized cargo load
ACU	Army combat uniform
ATTP	Army tactics, techniques, and procedures
BCT	brigade combat team
°C	degree Celsius
CIVD	cold induced vasodilation
CLP	cleaning, lubricating, and preservative compound
CONEX	container express
DA	Department of the Army
ECWCS	Extended Cold Weather Clothing System
°F	degree Fahrenheit
FM	field manual
FMFRP	fleet marine force reference publication
FMI	field manual-interim
G-4	assistant chief of staff, logistics
GPS	Global Positioning System
HMMWV	high mobility multipurpose wheeled vehicle
ISR	intelligence, surveillance, and reconnaissance
JP	joint publication
LAW	lubricating oil arctic, weapons
LOC	line of communications
LZ	landing zone
MCDP	Marine Corps doctrine publication
MCMWTC	Marine Corps Mountain Warfare Training Center
MCRP	Marine Corp reference publication
MCW	meal, cold weather
MCWP	Marine Corp warfighting publication
MED	medical
MRE	meal-ready-to-eat
MSTS	modular steel traction snowshoe
NiCd	nickel-cadmium
NiMH	nickel-metal hydride
PD	point detonating
PMCS	preventative maintenance checks and services
ROWPU	reverse osmosis water purification unit
S-4	logistics staff officer
SHA	space heater arctic
SUSV	small unit support vehicle (Marine Corps designation is BV-206)

TB	technical bulletin
TC	training circular
U.S.	United States
UN	United Nations
USMC	United States Marine Corps
VB	vapor barrier
VT	variable time

SECTION II – TERMS

civil support

Department of Defense support to U.S. civil authorities for domestic emergencies, and for designated law enforcement and other activities. (JP 3-28)

defensive operations

Combat operations conducted to defeat an enemy, attack, gain time, economize forces, and develop conditions favorable for offensive or stability operations. (FM 3-0)

fires warfighting function

The related tasks and systems that provide collective and coordinated Army indirect fires, joint fires, and command and control warfare, including nonlethal fires, through the targeting process. (FM 3-0) Those means used to delay, disrupt, degrade, or destroy enemy capabilities, forces, or facilities as well as affect the enemy's will to fight. (MCRP 5-12C)

maneuver warfighting function

The movement of forces for the purpose of gaining an advantage over the enemy. (MCRP 5-12C)

movement and maneuver warfighting function

The related tasks and systems that move forces to achieve a position of advantage in relation to the enemy. Direct fire is inherent in maneuver, as is close combat. (FM 3-0)

offensive operations

Combat operations conducted to defeat and destroy enemy forces and seize terrain, resources, and population centers. They impose the commander's will on the enemy. (FM 3-0)

stability operations

Various military missions, tasks, and activities conducted outside the United States in coordination with other instruments of power to maintain or reestablish a safe and secure environment, provide essential government services, emergency infrastructure reconstruction, and humanitarian relief. (JP 3-0)

sustainment warfighting function

The related tasks and systems that provide support and services to ensure freedom of action, extend operational reach, and prolong endurance. (FM 3-0)

tempo

The relative speed and rhythm of military operations over time with respect to the enemy. (FM 3-0)

References

Field manuals and selected joint publications are listed by new number followed by old number. An asterisk (*) marks those manuals that are dual designated.

REQUIRED PUBLICATIONS

These documents must be available to intended users of this publication.

FM 1-02 (101-5-1)/MCRP 5-12A. *Operational Terms and Graphics*. 21 September 2004.

JP 1-02. *Department of Defense Dictionary of Military and Associated Terms*. 8 November 2010.

MCDP 1-0. *Marine Corps Operations*. 27 September 2001.

RELATED PUBLICATIONS

These documents contain relevant supplemental information.

JOINT AND DEPARTMENT OF DEFENSE PUBLICATIONS

Most joint publications are available online: <http://www.dtic.mil/doctrine/new_pubs/jointpub.htm>.

JP 3-0. *Joint Operations*. 17 September 2006.

JP 3-28. *Civil Support*. 14 September 2007.

ARMY PUBLICATIONS

Most Army doctrinal publications are available online: <https://akocomm.us.army.mil/usapa/doctrine/Active_FM.html>. Army regulations are produced only in electronic media. Most are available online: < http://www.army mil/usapa/epubs/index html>.

AR 70-38. *Research, Development, Test, and Evaluation of Materiel for Extreme Climatic Conditions*. 15 September 1979.

FM 3-0. *Operations*. 27 February 2008.

FM 3-05.70. *Survival*. 17 May 2002.

FM 3-07. *Stability Operations*. 6 October 2008.

FM 3-11 (FM 3-100). *Multiservice Tactics, Techniques, and Procedures for Nuclear, Biological, and Chemical Defense Operations*. 10 March 2003.

FM 3-11.4 (FM 3-4). *Multiservice Tactics, Techniques, and Procedures for Nuclear, Biological, and Chemical (NBC) Protection*. 2 June 2003.

FM 3-11.9. *Potential Military Chemical/Biological Agents and Compounds*. 10 January 2005.

FM 3-13 (FM 100-6). *Information Operations: Doctrine, Tactics, Techniques, and Procedures*. 28 November 2003.

FM 3-21.8 (FM 7-8). *The Infantry Rifle Platoon and Squad*. 28 March 2007.

FM 3-28. *Civil Support Operations*. 20 August 2010.

FM 3-34. *Engineer Operations*. 2 April 2009.

FM 3-34.343 (FM 5-446). *Military Nonstandard Fixed Bridging*. 12 February 2002.

FM 3-50.3. *Survival, Evasion, and Recovery: Multi-Service Tactics, Techniques, and Procedures for Survival, Evasion, and Recovery*. 20 March 2007.

FM 3-90. *Tactics*. 4 July 2001.

*FM 3-90.12 (FM 90-13)/MCWP 3-17.1. *Combined Arms Gap-Crossing Operations*. 1 July 2008.

FM 3-97.6. *Mountain Operations*. 28 November 2000.

FM 3-97.61 (TC 90-6-1). *Military Mountaineering*. 26 August 2002.

FM 4-01.45. *Multi-Service Tactics, Techniques, and Procedures for Tactical Convoy Operations.* 13 January 2009.

FM 4-25.12 (FM 21-10-1). *Unit Field Sanitation Team.* 25 January 2002.

*FM 4-30.31 (FM 9-43-2)/ MCRP 4-11.4A (FMFRP 4-34). *Recovery and Battle Damage Assessment and Repair.* 19 September 2006.

FM 5-34. *Engineer Field Data.* 19 July 2005.

FM 5-102. *Countermobility.* 14 March 1985.

FM 5-103 (FM 5-15). *Survivability.* 10 June 1985.

FM 9-207. *Operation and Maintenance of Ordnance Materiel in Cold Weather.* 20 March 1998.

FM 10-52. *Water Supply in Theaters of Operations.* 11 July 1990.

*FM 21-10/MCRP 4-11.1D. *Field Hygiene and Sanitation.* 21 June 2000.

FM 90-7. *Combined Arms Obstacle Integration.* 29 September 1994.

FMI 4-93.2. *The Sustainment Brigade.* 4 February 2009.

TB MED 508. *Prevention and Management of Cold-Weather Injuries.* 1 April 2005.

TC 21-305-20 (FM 21-305). *Manual for the Wheeled Vehicle Operator.* 1 July 2009.

MARINE CORPS PUBLICATIONS

Most Marine Corps doctrinal publications are available online: <https://www.doctrine.quantico.usmc.mil/>.

MCRP 3-35.1A. *Small Unit Leader's Guide to Cold Weather Operations.* 8 October 2004.

MCRP 3-35.1B (FMFRP 7-25). *Instructor's Guide to Combat Skiing.* 23 December 2002.

MCRP 5-12C. *Marine Corps Supplement to the Department of Defense Dictionary of Military and Associated Terms.* 23 July 1998.

MCWP 3-17. *Engineering Operations.* 14 February 2000.

MCWP 3-40.2. *Information Management.* 24 January 2002.

MCWP 3-40.3. *MAGTF Communications System.* 8 January 2010.

MCWP 4-11. *Tactical-Level Logistics.* 13 June 2000.

MCWP 4-11.1. *Health Service Support Operations.* 10 March 1998.

MCWP 4-11.6. *Petroleum and Water Logistics Operations.* 19 June 2005.

OTHER PUBLICATIONS

Cold Weather (CWLC, CWOC & ALIT) Student Handout: Winter 2009-2010. Edition 9. United States Army Alaska Northern Warfare Training Center. November 2009. Available at http://www.wainwright.army.mil/nwtc/.

WEB SITES

Marine Corps Mountain Warfare Training Center at http://www.mwtc.usmc.mil/.

Northern Warfare Training Center at www.wainwright.army.mil/nwtc/.

United States Army Cold Regions Research and Engineering Laboratory <http://www.crrel.usace.army.mil/>

REFERENCED FORMS

DA Forms are available on the APD web site (www.apd.army.mil).

DA Form 2028. *Recommended Changes to Publications and Blank Forms.*

Index

Entries are by paragraph number.

This page intentionally left blank.

By Order of the Secretary of the Army:

GEORGE W. CASEY, JR.
General, United States Army
Chief of Staff

Official:

JOYCE E. MORROW
Administrative Assistant to the
Secretary of the Army
1100702

BY DIRECTION OF THE COMMANDANT OF THE MARINE CORPS:

GEORGE J. FLYNN
Lieutenant General, U.S. Marine Corps
Deputy Commandant for
Combat Development and Integration

DISTRIBUTION:

Active Army, Army National Guard, and U.S. Army Reserve: To be distributed in accordance with the initial distribution number 110313 requirements for ATTP 3-97.11/MCRP 3-35.1D.

www.ingramcontent.com/pod-product-compliance
Lightning Source LLC
Chambersburg PA
CBHW080207300326
41934CB00038B/3398